SATELLITE
MARKETING™
USING SOCIAL MEDIA TO
CREATE ENGAGEMENT

KEVIN POPOVIĆ

CRC Press
Taylor & Francis Group
Boca Raton London New York

CRC Press is an imprint of the
Taylor & Francis Group, an **informa** business

CRC Press
Taylor & Francis Group
6000 Broken Sound Parkway NW, Suite 300
Boca Raton, FL 33487-2742

© 2016 by Kevin Popovic
CRC Press is an imprint of Taylor & Francis Group, an Informa business

No claim to original U.S. Government works

Printed on acid-free paper
Version Date: 20151209

International Standard Book Number-13: 978-1-4822-5614-7 (Paperback)

This book contains information obtained from authentic and highly regarded sources. Reasonable efforts have been made to publish reliable data and information, but the author and publisher cannot assume responsibility for the validity of all materials or the consequences of their use. The authors and publishers have attempted to trace the copyright holders of all material reproduced in this publication and apologize to copyright holders if permission to publish in this form has not been obtained. If any copyright material has not been acknowledged please write and let us know so we may rectify in any future reprint.

Library of Congress Cataloging-in-Publication Data

Popovic, Kevin, 1964-
    Satellite marketing : using social media for improving customer participation and engagement / Kevin Popovic.
        pages cm
    Includes bibliographical references and index.
    ISBN 978-1-4822-5614-7 (paperback)
    1. Internet marketing. 2. Customer relations. 3. Social media. 4. Marketing--Social aspects. I. Title.

HF5415.1265.P66 2016
658.8'72--dc23   2015019603

Visit the Taylor & Francis Web site at
http://www.taylorandfrancis.com

and the CRC Press Web site at
http://www.crcpress.com

Dedicated to my father, Dr. Charles Popovich, for the lessons in marketing and the relentless encouragement. I would not be the marketer I am today without you. Thanks, Pops.

Thank you.

I want to thank Rodney Rumford (@Rumford) for introducing me to the blogosphere and teaching me what he knows about social media. Rodney was there at the beginning of Satellite Marketing, and he invited me to share my theories at the Gravity Summit Social Media Conference at UCLA in 2010. Rodney said he would only let me present if I was going to write the book, so I promised him I would. Rodney, here's the damn book.

I want to thank George Evans from Brandwidth for being my creative muse and sometimes editor. Sometimes he would help me and sometimes he wouldn't, but he has always been there when I needed him, and he makes me better. Thanks, Georgie.

There are numerous people on my creative team at Ideahaus that have helped with the development of this book over the years– thanks to all for doing your part. There are a couple who deserve special recognition:

Jeff Wood worked with me to create our visual approach to the material and the cover art. It didn't work until it worked, and that's why I've worked with him for 20-some years. Thanks for your commitment to creativity, Jeffy.

Hunter Homistek (@HunterAHomistek) was our editor, making sure my rants made sense and that we passed academic muster. Thanks for your diligence, Hunter.

Of course, thank you to my clients - the good people who have invested in my services and that provided me an opportunity to develop my work. I am so very grateful.

Lastly, I'd like to thank my wife, Petra, and my daughter, Charlie, for their patience during this book. There were a lot of times I was with the book and not them – my apologies. I promise I won't write another book without asking first. - kp

Kevin Popović, Author. Photo by Cece Canton.

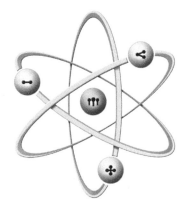

@SATELLITEMKTG

This book answers the question we've all asked, "How can my business leverage social media to create engagement?"

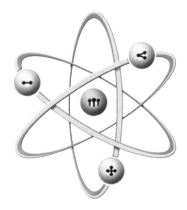

On Creating Engagement

Remember when businesses were built by personal engagement with customers? I do.

Picture graciously provided from the personal collection of Daniel Jackson.

My grandmother sold shoes for a living. For 30 years families went to see Dorothy Popović at Jackson's Shoe Store in Hopewell, Pennsylvania, every time they needed a pair of shoes: a church holiday, the first day of school, a wedding, a new outfit, a high school dance, or the first job interview. Founded in 1925*, Jackson's also had other stores in other neighborhoods, but Dorothy took care of hers. Whenever somebody needed shoes, they went to see "Dot."

Mothers were confident that Dorothy would make sure their ever-growing children got the right size—it's what she did. Men trusted Dorothy to get them a pair of boots that were comfortable and would hold up to the mill floor—that's who she was. Kids looked forward to riding on the Buster Brown pedal carousel after they were done trying on multiple colors of Keds®. Each customer had a relationship with their salesperson, and it meant something —to both of them. That's what you got when you went to Jackson's.

Then something started to change. Chain stores headquartered in other cities came to town and offered lower prices than Jackson's, and some of the customers followed the money. Dorothy still did what she did: She listened to her customers and helped them find the shoes they needed.

As the number of local shoe stores grew, so did the number of sales and promotions from the manufacturers. The shoe companies would pick a line of shoes, suggest a promotion or sales strategy to generate more interest in the product to create more traffic, and the sales people were incentivized to participate—including my grandmother.

A few years later, the area got its first big mall, and it attracted curious shoppers from all over the region, including many of Dorothy's customers. Some bought shoes from the department stores that sold just about everything, including shoes. There were styles Jackson's didn't have, and many of her customers tried them because they were on sale or advertised in the newspaper. She continued with what she knew: helping people.

Jackson's closed the Hopewell store and moved into the mall to compete—carousel and all. The big stores had big sales and were staffed by many, many people, most of whom did not know the families or the children or the shoes. But they did know how to ring the new registers, how to send customers to the other departments, and how to get them to open a store credit card.

The department store office would use the customer information from the charge accounts to market other things to the new customers. The store would send them letters in the mail from big databases on spinning reels of tape that sometimes read, "Dear <first_name>," as if they knew to whom they were selling.

Kevin Popović with his grandmother Dorothy

Dot was getting older—near 60 at this point. Although some of the children of her longtime customers would bring their children into the store to meet her, to share a story about getting shoes when they were a child, and to ride the now very worn carousel, it wasn't the same. Neither was the money she made.

Sales were off, margins were down, and nobody seemed to be in retail as a profession any longer. It was a part-time job or something that was done when somebody got laid-off or while they were working on their next big idea. There was no customer engagement—only numbered accounts, computers merging big data with form fields and bulk postage filling the sales funnel to move the inventory purchased by remote buyers.

For the committed sales professional, it was tough too: matching prices, coupons, buy-one-get-one sales, and the never-ending allure of the well-branded department stores. Their options were limited. They had a telephone, but who wanted to be bothered at dinner? They had the postal service, but who was reading mail? They had their reputations, but the distance between interactions slowly diminished the impact they had on a customer-buying decision.

Well, relationships are changing—again.

Social media is providing the ability to engage customers as businesses used to engage customers: by first name, asking about their kids, and knowing something about them from the last time you spoke.

Social Media and The Return of the Customer Relationship

Social media has become ubiquitous. It transcends age, gender and geography. As of June 2015, Facebook has 1.49 billion active users (Statista.com 2015) and Twitter has 316 million active users. LinkedIn has reported 380,000,000 in 2015 (LinkedIn 2015).

But social media is more than Facebook, Twitter, LinkedIn and YouTube. Social media encompasses social bookmarking, slideshares, podcasts, blogs, user-powered news sites, forums, check-in apps, product and service reviews, email newsletters and more. If people are sharing information and engaging in conversations through some form of technology, they are using social media.

Businesses worldwide see this gathering of consumers who voluntarily segment themselves into niche groups as marketing opportunities. Sixty-five percent of the world's top companies maintain a Twitter presence. Ninety percent of marketers use social media channels for business, and 72% of experienced social media marketers (three or more years working in the medium) see a boost in turnover because of social media (*Pring, 2012*). This shift is likely occurring because consumers are less trusting in paid advertising and more in "earned" advertising, which the *2012 Global Trust in Advertising Survey* confirms.

Randall Beard, global head, Advertiser Solutions at Nielsen, says, "Although television advertising will remain a primary way marketers connect with audiences due to its unmatched reach compared to other media, consumers around the world continue to see recommendations from friends, colleagues and co-workers and online consumer opinions as by far the most credible. As a result, successful brand advertisers will seek ways to better connect with consumers and leverage their goodwill in the form of consumer feedback and experiences" (Grimes, *2012*).

Social media is the ideal tool for leveraging online consumer opinions. A community that is actively engaged with a brand will say positive things about products, both in the form of formal product reviews as well as through more casual channels, such as posts, comments and likes, which can spill over into word-of-mouth support. For business-to-business (B2B) marketing, these facts and figures continue to apply, as the ultimate goal of B2B marketing is to influence key decision makers within a business. According to the 2012 Social Media Marketing Industry Report, 93% of B2B marketers use social media to market their businesses, up from 88% in 2010 (Mershon, *2012*). The survey also noted that B2B marketers tend to be veteran social media marketers, having three or more years of experience over business-to-consumer (B2C) marketers (Mershon, *2012*).

The research demonstrates that social media is a powerful tool for brands working both in B2C and in B2B, and chances are that if you are not on social media, your competitors are (Formalarie, 2012). Social media marketing is no longer an option. It's a must.

What This Book Is Not

This book is not theoretical. I will not use pretend names and cities or call something a widget for lack of a more accurate name.

This book is not about Facebook. It is not about Twitter or LinkedIn or YouTube or any other specific social media site or service or channel.

This book is not about how to make viral videos (because you can't make a viral video, only a large number of people that watch a video can make a video "go viral," or to spread like a virus).

This book is not about any secrets or shortcuts because there are no secrets. You can know everything you need to know and there are still no shortcuts. You just have to do the work.

What This Book Is

This book is strategic. This book shares how we have come to learn to successfully use social media to engage with people. We share our actionable process, field-tested since 2007 and improved with knowledge gained from each project to which it has been applied.

This book will share with you my perspective of how things work, what is required to be successful and what I have learned about social media from my real-world experience as a professional, an educator and a thought leader.

In the end, this book provides a thorough understanding of social media, its potential for creating engagement, and a demonstration of a complete process for application.

How To Read This Book

This book has been written to provide the information you need to understand social media in the context of communications, in the order in which I believe it should be addressed. The process is based on the understanding we have of social media, as well as what we have learned from other types of communications, and has been structured into what I believe are logical steps.

The exercises at the end of each step in the process are designed to immediately apply what you have just read to something important to you: your business. This creates learning. Doing so after each step clarifies your thoughts about the requirements of each step and helps you move forward with engaging your audience.

Use the Glosary to better understand words you do not understand, and to confirm those where you are unsure. Use the Index to help you identify all of the resources within the book.

References

Beaver County Times (Jan. 31, 1969). *Jackson Shoe Head Is Named:*
  As retrieved: *http://news.google.com/newspapers?nid=2002&dat=19660127&id=M PUuAAAIBAJ&sjid=rtsFAAAAIBJ&pg=1718,5203352*
Bennett, S. (21 March 2012). Twitter Now Has More Than 140 Million Active Users Sending 340 Million Tweets Every Day. *Media Bistro.* http://www.mediabistro.com/alltwitter/twitter-140-million-active-users_ b19729
Bennett, S. (1 Nov. 2012). Facebook, Twitter, Pinterest, Instagram Social Media Statistics and Facts 2012 [INFOGRAPHIC]. *Media Bistro.* http://www.mediabistro.com/alltwitter/social-media-stats-2012_b30651
Grimes, M. (10 April 2012). Nielsen: Global Consumers' Trust in 'Earned' Advertising Grows in Importance. *Nielsen.* Retrieved from: http://www.nielsen.com/us/en/insights/press-room/2012/nielsen-global-consumers-trust-in-earned-advertising-grows.html

Mershon, P. (24 April 2012). How B2B Marketers Use Social Media: New Research. *Social Media Examiner.* Retrieved from:

    http://www.socialmediaexaminer.com/b2b-social-media-marketing-research/

Pring, C. (10 May 2012). 99 New Social Media Stats for 2012. *The Social Skinny.*

    http://thesocialskinny.com/99-new-social-media-stats-for-2012/

YouTube (2012). Statistics. *YouTube: Press Room.* Retrieved from: http://www.youtube.com/t/press_statistics

Yung-Hui, L. (30 Sept. 2012). 1 Billion Facebook Users on Earth: Are We There Yet? *Forbes.* http://www.forbes.com/sites/limyunghui/2012/09/30/1-billion-facebook-users-on-earth-are-we-there-yet/

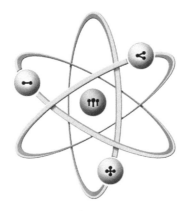

ABOUT THE AUTHOR

Context For Perspective

Kevin Popović teaching a social media workshop at the World Resources SIM Center, San Diego. Photo by Cece Canton.

Founder, Author, Speaker, Teacher.

Kevin Popović is the founder of Ideahaus®, an award-winning creative communications agency that helps its clients figure out what to say and how to say it to build brands and increase sales. With more than 30 years of professional experience, he helps make strategic decisions about all types of business communications, facilitates the creative process, and demonstrates how to best manage resources to generate a return on each investment.

As an academic, Popović earned a B.A. in communications / psychology, an M.S. in multimedia technology, and focused doctoral studies within instructional technologies. He has developed curricula for creative, communications and business courses and has taught undergraduate, graduate, and continuing education, as well as developed and delivered corporate training for Fortune 500 companies.

Popović's most recent academic research article, "Attitudes on the Use of Social Media in Healthcare Communications," published in the *Journal of Communications in Healthcare* (2013 Vol. 6 No. 1), assessed current attitudes of healthcare, pharmaceutical and life sciences executives on the topic. His preceding article, "Tweeting @DrWelby: Practical Examples of Social Media in Healthcare" (2010 Vol. 3 No. 2), was one of the first to explore the use of social media in healthcare communications.

Popović is also the author of *20 YEARS Communications: 20 Leaders, 20 Questions, 100's of Lessons.* Twenty leaders from different corners of the industry answer 20 questions on the evolution of communications, providing insight to where communications was, is, and will go. A thought-provoking learning tool, *20YEARS Communications* is designed to generate discussion and critical analysis–ideal for the classroom, for team building, and for professional communicators looking to expand their perspective.

In 2010, Popović was ranked #43 in Fast Company's *The Influence Project,* measuring the "most influential people online." In 2014 and 2015, Online Marketing Institute named him one of the "Top 20 Digital Strategists in Marketing" and one of the "15 Most Influential Educators in Digital Marketing."

Popović currently teaches Creativity & Innovation in the School of Mangement for the College of Business at San Diego State University. He serves on the Board of Advisers for the Lavin Entrepreneurship Program and is an active mentor in the program.

Engage with "KP" on Twitter @KevinPopovic, like on Facebook, or connect on LinkedIn.

"Satellite Marketing" became a way to illustrate a strategy based on goals, and establish a process to create an actionable plan.

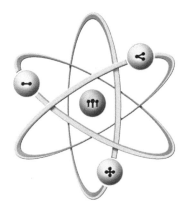

CHAPTER ONE

Origins of Satellite Marketing

The Origins of Satellite Marketing

In October of 2006, our agency was contracted to produce a video documentary for a startup. The business was called MojoPages, one of the first consumer-rated service directories online (think Yellow Pages with comments and rating stars) from the people who used their services, like Angie's List or Yelp.

The working title of the project was *"30 Days To Launch: Behind the Scenes of a Startup*."* The idea was simple: Produce a weekly program showcasing the behind-the-scenes efforts of a group of young entrepreneurs in Southern California as they move from concept to corporation. "30 Days to Launch" had all the makings of a reality show by design—a cast of characters, a luxury beachfront set, and a storyline about making millions. Instead of an on-air broadcast, the video series would be available from video-sharing sites, such as YouTube, Veoh, and Vimeo. An audience scattered across the Internet could watch MojoPages start its company from the ground up in only 30 days to build their brand recognition, attract partners and investors, and, perhaps, get famous along the way.

My role began as cameraman / producer / director—an embedded reporter capturing the behind-the-scenes action of the organization in daily crisis. I would also capture the drama (yes, drama) of five men coming together to build a company under the leadership of a blonde-haired boy wonder (you're welcome, Jon Carder).

Viewers could watch an episode the day it "aired" (became available on the site) or on-demand (when their schedules permitted). They could watch it themselves or with their friends, they could share the link with a colleague, and they could engage by leaving comments on the video for the characters in the show. The content was always available.

In addition to the weekly videos we were responsible for producing, publicist Ray Drasnin was hired to approach the media for news coverage. Ray's job was to develop an idea for a story, dial every TV and print editor on a well-crafted list of media outlets, then pitch with a furious vengeance until someone told him they would do a story on MojoPages. With our shows being hosted on video-sharing sites, Ray shared a link to the video assets for his e-mail pitch to the media. Editors appreciated seeing what Ray was talking about during his phone pitch and getting to know the people behind the story before they committed to sharing MojoPages with their respective audiences, to which they did.

Rodney Rumford was an early pioneer of the Internet and was contracted to create interest from what, at the time, was called "the blogosphere." The Internet's version of the media, Rodney was leveraging his relationships with the writers and editors of the more popular blogs to help tell the MojoPages story online. Rodney shared the link to the videos with the bloggers he was pitching for the same reason—exposing the new business to new people. When bloggers bought into our storyline, they embedded (shared) our video episodes into their blog posts to share with their audience.

In our individual efforts, we were able to accomplish our expected goals. Some people watched our videos, some of the media wrote about MojoPages, and some bloggers wrote about the new idea for an online company. Like many people, you may be interested to learn how they were able to launch an online company—including securing the funding—in only 30 days.

They didn't.

What was supposed to take 30 days took more than 120, and a contract for four episodes turned into an extension to produce 14. On week five, we started planning further in advance because it didn't look like this was going to be just another week or two.

As we continued planning our individual efforts, building off the best practices we were learning, we began seeing patterns in what we had accomplished. Ray got CEO Jon Carder placed on the cover of *Fortune Small Business.* Rodney got a blogger to write a post about the front cover. I included Jon thanking Fortune Magazine and the blogger for covering MojoPages in our video. We changed these typically one-to-one closed connections into an infinite loop of open communication, which, as we discovered, kept everyone talking (perpetually) about the other.

A blogger would write about MojoPages, saying "thanks" for the mention in the video. Then, the media would write about the support we were getting from the bloggers, and we would thank the new list of supporters in the next video. Each of our singular audiences was interested in the content from the others. The more we continued with this cycle of integrated communication, the more momentum we created for the business, and the more media coverage MojoPages received, and the more support we received online.

There was something to this. People were engaged.

MojoPages was transparent, by design, which meant we shared everything with the public. From the CEO's vision, to the concerns with the COO—even the challenges getting funding from the CFO—our audience saw it all from us first on YouTube, as it happened. They saw the people behind the titles; they got to know them—faults and all, they saw the success and failure, and the audience trusted them for doing so.

With each new episode, we created opportunities for MojoPages; we attracted new partners, investors knew our pitch before we showed up, and users were counting down the days until we opened for business. What we would soon realize was that we discovered how to create engagement—an interaction between MojoPages and their audience. By integrating multi-media content with traditional public relations tactics and the growing Internet community, we created word-of-mouth with all our target audiences. We were getting MojoPages in front of the right people, and the numbers proved it. Partners were not only open to deals, but they were making them. Investors were not only taking our meetings, but they were investing.

And before we even launched MojoPages, we had a higher Alexa Internet rating (web traffic analysis) than any of our competitors already open for business.

Mission accomplished. Or was it?

Admittedly, in 2006 this strategy wasn't something we had used before—it was a new tactic with a new ingredient: the Internet. Sure, our client was ecstatic that the strategy worked, but as a marketer and an academic, I wanted to learn why it worked. If we could repeat this success for other clients, in other markets, we would have something of great value.

Why It Worked

In 2009, a Nielsen "Trust in Advertising Report* was released which helped shed some light on why we had been so successful creating engagement: "Global advertising consumers trust real friends and virtual strangers the most." Word-of-mouth was identified as "the most powerful selling tool" available.

Recommendations from people who knew MojoPages created more trust (90%) among the people they knew than any other type of advertising. The positive comments people were posting online generated the second highest amount of trust (70%) among people they did not know. The MojoPages website, which included daily insights from every department of the company, statistically generated as much trust (70%) as the editorial content from news-papers, magazine, television and radio (69%). We surrounded our audience with the four most effective types of advertising, and it worked.

The strategy for MojoPages created engagement because people were talking about MojoPages. People wrote good things, people read what other people wrote and then wrote more positive comments; more people read those. What the audiences read about the company they liked, what they saw in the videos about the people who were creating the company they talked about, and everyone wanted to see them succeed because they felt like they each had a little stake in it all. And they did.

Where Satellites Come From

With the public success of MojoPages, I was asked by a client to present what we learned about social media for business as a lecture to a conference of educators. With the emergence of social media as a communications channel, most businesses were very interested in learning what it was and how it worked—even schools. As a business looking

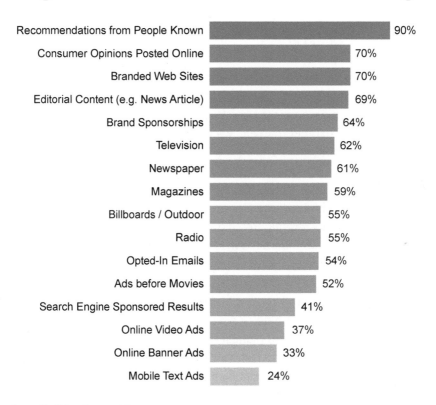

Degrees of Trust in Forms of Advertising

Recommendations from People Known	90%
Consumer Opinions Posted Online	70%
Branded Web Sites	70%
Editorial Content (e.g. News Article)	69%
Brand Sponsorships	64%
Television	62%
Newspaper	61%
Magazines	59%
Billboards / Outdoor	55%
Radio	55%
Opted-In Emails	54%
Ads before Movies	52%
Search Engine Sponsored Results	41%
Online Video Ads	37%
Online Banner Ads	33%
Mobile Text Ads	24%

Source: The Nielsen Company 4-09

for ways to engage with the early adopting student demographic, social media was of particular interest to those in admissions (aka, sales).

In the audience would be the CEOs, VPs and management of the attending schools, most technologically capable (at worst), familiar with the conventional marketing of their business and aware of the emergence of a new "social" media. There would also be owners, board members and trustees in attendance, most in their sixties and seventies, who did not have a comfort level with technology and surely would have no idea about anything called "social media."

Admittedly, I was a bit perplexed. How could I best explain social media, let alone the strategic use of content marketing for engaging prospective students, to an audience as old as my grandfather? I needed to draw an analogy for them, for everyone—even myself—to better explain how this was working and why it was important to their business.

I titled my presentation, "The State of Communications - How Social Media Changed the Way We Communicate," to introduce the new subject matter in context and was intent on keeping this simple. I even used the PowerPoint template that looks like a chalkboard to make the material more familiar to the educators in my audience.

After I was introduced, I surveyed my audience, "How many people use social media?" Roughly half of the audience raised their hands. My follow-up, "How many people have no idea what social media is?" raised the other hands, mostly the older audience who concerned me in the first place.

I started with what they all knew: There were many different types of people that the school wanted to speak with, for different reasons.

• Prospects	• Parents	• Employers	• Media
• Students	• Staff	• Industry	• Owners
• Alumni	• Faculty	• Government	• Management

Next, I revisited each type of person to discuss how we could reach them using conventional marketing. "In the past," I started, "to connect with prospective students, the schools used conventional marketing tools, like open house events, word-of-mouth referrals from alumni and current students, presentation opportunities to students in high schools, print brochures, print ads in local papers, an 800-number and direct mail."

I shared current statistics on how each was performing, shared some examples of the work our agency had produced and added a little personality until I got all of the heads in the audience nodding up and down with the things I was saying.

Then I introduced social media, the different types of social media (in no particular order) that were available (at this time), and I told them that each could serve as potential channels of communication to create engagement.

- Social Networks
- Micro-blogging
- Events

- Bookmarks
- Blogging
- Photo Sharing

- PPT Sharing
- Video Sharing
- Widgets

- Miscellaneous

I compared what they were already doing to reach students with how they could use social media to reach students.

"With social media," I continued, "your business is now able to reach prospects directly, online, where they are already organized with their friends and in the groups in which they already participate. The school can share posts about upcoming events with links to maps and directions. Admissions can even repurpose online user reviews to deliver credible email marketing." I even showed pictures of everything I was talking about right after I talked about it to help them understand.

That's when the older audience stopped nodding.

I worked my way over to the older gentlemen seated together in the front row, two of whom were wearing American flags on their lapel, just like my grandfather used to wear. Their pins reminded me of him, and I thought, "How would I explain social media to my grandfather?"

I thought: Satellites.

I asked, "How many of you gentlemen served in the military?" Almost all of them raised their hands. I grabbed a few erasable markers from the podium and worked my way to the whiteboard.

"Who remembers Sputnik?" Hands went in the air. I asked, "What was Sputnik?" No immediate answers were offered, so I gestured to the man closest to me and he answered, "Well, it was a satellite."

I said, "Right. It was a satellite. And what did that satellite do when it was overtop the U.S?"

"It spied on us!" one replied. "Yeah," I said. "It spied on us."

I walked over to the whiteboard and drew a circle in the middle of the screen, like the Earth, and drew three circles around the outside, like orbital paths every kid has seen since fifth-grade science. I drew a line straight up from the center and an arrow where the line met each path.

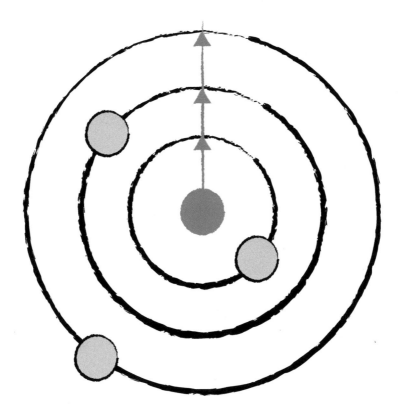

"The Russians put a satellite in orbit that circled the Earth and spied on the U.S. every day. At some point in the day, that satellite had a line of sight over the top of us and was able to see what we're doing, right?" Heads nodded faster. My veteran audience was buying into this satellite analogy.

Then I drew three small circles on each of the three orbits, each a different size and each with a different distance from the center.

"After they had put their satellite in orbit to watch us, we put one in orbit to watch them, and then the Chinese followed after us. At some point, every day, we encountered one of those satellites, right?" All of the heads were nodding.

I continued by explaining they could think of social media for business as different types of satellites, or marketing "sub-stations," that moved much faster than traditional media. Satellites are built for specific purposes or utilize a needed technology and offer smaller, faster, more dynamic communication opportunities than conventional marketing.

At some point most every day, these satellites would come into range of our prospects and be able to provide data to them, establish first contact with us and help us to communicate with each other. There would be something about these satellites that would attract our audience to engage—messages from people at the school, pictures from students, videos from events, links to other web pages with calendars and applications. Most days, people in our audience were attracted to this content and were compelled to participate in these online communities.

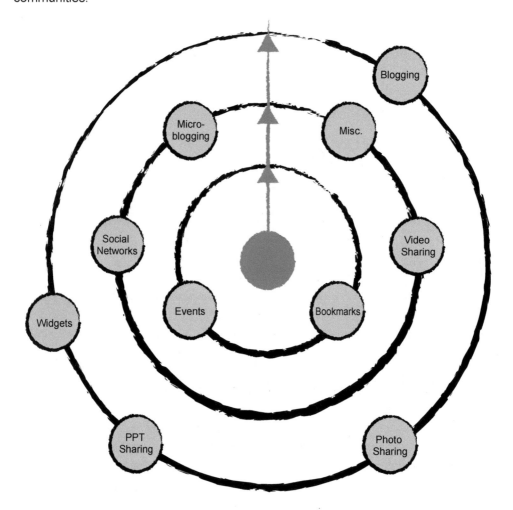

Original concept of Satellite Marketing™ diagram denoting different types of social media with varying relevance to the target market (2006).

I suggested that social media could help the school engage with its audience on the social media channels where they were already available.

Social media "satellites" can supplement traditional media, such as print, radio, television, direct mail and outdoor advertising. They can support existing business communications, such as marketing, customer support and sales. As I shared in my MojoPages story, social media (like video sharing and blogs) could not only integrate into conventional marketing communications (like public relations), but could increase the efficacy of the effort.

The metaphor of satellites seemed to make sense to everyone in the audience, and to me. It was a way to frame the concept that allowed users to visualize what it meant to their business. The graphics made it easier to remember how social media worked, to understand that each satellite was different from each other, and to identify how these non-business channels could be used for business.

If the goal is to expand the reach of the organization and enhance the results by creating relationships, then social media was a new option. "Satellite Marketing" became a way to illustrate the concept, develop a strategy based on goals, and establish a process to create an actionable plan.

Social media is interesting, but satellites have a purpose.

References

MojoPages: 30 Days to Launch: Video Documentary Series Intro. (2006, October 26). Retrieved December 14, 2014, from http://youtu.be/0VcausWLURY

GLOBAL ADVERTISING CONSUMERS TRUST REAL FRIENDS AND VIRTUAL STRANGERS THE MOST. (2009, July 7). Retrieved December 14, 2014, from http://www.nielsen.com/us/en/insights/news/2009/global-adverting-consumers-trust-real-friends-and-virtual-strangers-the-most.html

GLOBAL TRUST IN ADVERTISING AND BRAND MESSAGES. (2013, September 17). Retrieved December 14, 2014, from http://www.nielsen.com/us/en/news wire/2013/under-the-influence-consumer-trust-in-advertising.html

Popovic, K. (Director) (2009, March 27). "The State of Communications" or "How Social Media Changed the Way We Communicate". Educators Conference 2009. Lecture conducted from Pittsburgh Technical Institute, Pittsburgh, PA. Retrieved from: http://www.slideshare.net/ideahaus/ptistateofcommunications

"Identifying that next big thing, before the competition, can mean the difference between being a market leader or a never-was."

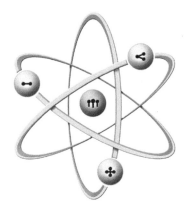

CHAPTER TWO

The Evolution of Marketing

My father was a professor of marketing at Robert Morris University, and my uncle was an international business consultant. Every Sunday at my grandmother's dinner table, I would hear them share client stories, discuss strategy, and debate their adaptation of "The 5 P's of Marketing*"—product, price, promotion, place, and people. Every company, according to my father, would develop their strategy by mixing these elements to create a differential advantage (i.e., make them different than their competition) in the eyes of the customers in the marketplace.

My grandfather, having left the table after his meal at the start of these discussions, would watch the Pittsburgh Steelers (or the Pirates—depending on the time of year) on a black-and-white television with no sound. Instead of using the television audio, a single ear bud from his pocket radio tuned to KDKA-AM Sports Talk. In his lap, covered in ash from two packs of Marlboro Lights, was the sports section of the *Pittsburgh Post-Gazette*. This detail will be important later.

The 5 P's Marketing Mix

Product	Price	Promotion	Place	People
Pt 01	**Pc** 02	**Pr** 03	**Pl** 04	**Pe** 05

This "marketing mix," as my father taught, was a term coined by Harvard Business School Advertising Professor Neil Borden in 1948*. It focused on what the company had to offer to the consumer. The product—goods or services—refers to all of the features and benefits the company creates. The price included not only the price tag of the product (retail), but also the cost to manufacture. It included the profit margin between the company and resellers (wholesale), and any (sales) discounts needed to maintain a competitive advantage. Promotion included all of the activities needed to make customers aware of goods and services in the marketplace, like packaging, advertising, sales, public relations, etc. The place is where the product is produced, distributed, or made available to the consumer. If you're a retailer, it's your store, and as my father taught me, it included three key elements: location, location and location.

The last "P" was people—not the people who buy your product, but the people who make your product, sell it, and support it in the marketplace. This was the one "P" I was always confused about. How is this not about the people who buy the product?

4 P's, 7 P's, 8 P's–More?

In 1960, another marketing professor, E.J. McCarthy, discarded "people" altogether in his "Basic Marketing: A Managerial Approach," reducing the mix to only product, price, promotion and place*. Perhaps McCarthy did not discard it as much as he simply did not include it, but I could never find anything that told me one way or the other. Given the 5 P's which came first, one may assume discarded.

The 4 P's were later expanded to 7 P's by Booms and Bitner in 1981*. As services became more prevalent, they added back the "people" who delivered the services, as well as the "process" representing the mechanisms and procedures for delivery. They even took it a step further and threw in "physical evidence" the service had been delivered (proof to the consumer that they got what they paid for).

Later, seven would grow to 8 P's in 2007 as Lovelock and Wirtz* argued "productivity" was another critical element in "Services Marketing: People, Technology, Strategy." Since Lovelock and Wirtz focused on the consumer and competitive environments in services marketing, this could explain the addition of "productivity"—a metric for measuring the return on investment (ROI) of their management plan.

What were they all seeing in their theories? From my perspective, everything except the people they were trying to reach.

A Consumer-Oriented Model

In 1990, the same year I started my agency, Bob Lauterborn introduced the "4 C's" in an *Advertising Age* article titled: "Four P's Passe; C-words Take Over." Lauterborn, a professor of advertising and a former director of marketing communications, observed the disconnect advertising and marketing has had to work through. He said, "The trouble with our newly minted MBA's is that they're well-prepared for a world which no longer exists."

The 4 C's Consumer-Oriented Model

Consumer	Cost	Convenience	Communication
Cr 01	**Ct** 02	**Ce** 03	**Cn** 04

Lauterborn replaces "product" with "consumer," suggesting the company study what the consumer "wants and needs," not what the company produces. Price is replaced with "cost," as the price to produce the product is only part of the equation the consumer considers when evaluating a purchasing decision. Place has become less relevant than ever and "convenience" more than ever as new methods of communications, payment ,and delivery better serve the changing lifestyle and consumption of consumers.

Lastly, promotion was replaced with "communication." In Lauterborn's view, Promotion is manipulative, while Advertising "creates a dialog" between the company and the consumer "which may be the formula for success as we leave the second millennium."

Consumer, cost, convenience, communication: Lauterborn's forward thinking would better fit the movement for many companies from mass marketing to niche marketing, selling only what the consumer wants to buy. The 4 C's would be viewed by many, including myself, as a common-sense consumer-oriented model*, shifting the focus from the company to the consumer.

The Evolution of Marketing Communications

Marketers have historically worked to get noticed in the marketplace—it's the nature of their role on the team. And like any other work, there have been tools created to complete specific tasks.

From the design of a laborer's mark to the branding of an institution, there has been a need to distinguish one company from another. From the simple poster advertising a product to the goodwill and relations with the public, there has been a need to communicate with the community at large. As the market grew crowded, marketing promotions became necessary to get the consumers' attention. Requirements for "bigger" and "new" often included technology just recently adopted for mass communication.

Identifying that next big thing, before the competition, can mean the difference between being a market leader or a never-was.

The Use of Technology in Marketing Communications

In my article, "Predicting the Digital Marketing Future: Learn from the Analog Past*," we learn how the advancements in technology over the years have helped marketers reach more customers in pursuit of market share. These improvements and changes have dramatically impacted the opportunities for outbound marketing—marketing messages that are broadcast, aka "multiplied," to reach more consumers.

Identifying the right technology is half of the formula; knowing when to adopt is the other. Too early and nobody gets it. Too late and nobody cares. Remember the guy with the first fax machine? He couldn't wait for the second guy to buy one.

History recounts the origin of the tools we have developed for marketing communications over the last 600 years. It also provides insight into how to create a marketing channel. By examining all of these channels and identifying any patterns in their history, we can learn what we should expect as we look to the digital future.

The Technology of Print

When Gutenberg invented the printing press in 1450, he invented "mass communications." Suddenly one message could be multiplied, replacing verbal communications and the need to tell a story over and over and over again. Even though print was new and innovative, adoption was slow. The masses didn't have access to the technology (books) or they didn't know how to use it (how to read) so they could not use books to communicate. Not until the technology became widespread, easily accessible, and people learned to use it (read and write) could print reach critical mass and become a tool for communication.

Three hundred years later (1730), print magazines emerged as the first public media, enabling businesses to promote themselves within a collection of public content to a subscriber base of literate consumers. Repurposed print advertising emerged as larger-poster advertising in 1839 and was adopted by businesses to smaller public spaces with high traffic and frequency. Larger billboard advertising wasn't available for rent for another 30 years (1867). Over time, people got used to the technology, and business models that demonstrated opportunity meeting application emerged, generating profitability (ROI) for business investment in the medium and revenue for the technology provider.

Lessons from Print

- No matter how interesting or unique, until the technology becomes widespread and accessible by the masses, it will not become a media communications channel.
- Media splinters: What starts at one divides, then these divisions are replicated by competition.
- Message content can adapt to any container.

• Over time, models will emerge that demonstrate best practices and ROI.

New Media

In 1876, Alexander Graham Bell patented a "new" type of medium called the telephone—an "apparatus for transmitting vocal or other sounds telegraphically"—connecting two people over a wire from a distance. "Wireless telegraphy" connected one-to-many 44 years later in 1920, using radio to cover a greater distance with an antenna. Six years later, in 1926, television transmitted sound with moving pictures.

Like print, radio created a marketing vehicle for business via sponsored content (1922), but it took the U.S. Federal Communications Commission (FCC) until 1941–15 years—to license the use of the channels. In order to qualify for a license, the FCC required public service programming commitments in order to allow stations to broadcast commercial advertisements. New models for new media came faster than print, although it was nearly a century before telemarketing emerged as a strategic use of the telephone in 1970.

Lessons from New Media

• "New" media is a subjective term—there's always something new.
• The evolution of a new technology into a new media channel takes time.
• Regulation does not respond at the same rate at which technology arises.
• Timing is everything.

From Analog to Digital

In 1972, 500 years after its invention, print was declared dead (for the first time). Television—the newest new medium—was suspected as the culprit. The Buggles also indicted television in 1979, declaring, "Video Killed the Radio Star."

A year later (1973), digital was born as the mobile (handheld) phone, and people began connecting on the move. Eight years later (1981), personal computers helped marketers manage consumer data on a PC, and within three years, we were all managing data and creating digital content on a Mac (1984). Technology multiplied—again—to provide more for the mass communications via desktop publishing (1985) and SMS messaging (1990) on the millions of increasingly functional phones. The same scale came to television in 1990 as satellite TV brought more channels of content to a larger geographic audience on-demand.

Lessons from Digital

- Technology moves forward, never in reverse.
- The consumer is mobile and accessible.
- Digital content does not cost to replicate.
- The consumer's data are readily available to make informed decisions and to deliver targeted messaging.

Enter the Internet

In late 1989, Tim Berners-Lee, an English computer scientist, invented the World Wide Web—a system of interlinked hypertext documents accessed via the Internet we have come to know as Web pages. Only two years after academia adapted this new medium (1992), marketing interjected (spam) messages (1994) within their message board content. Internet directories created to catalog content (1994) initiated search-engine marketing strategies (1995) to influence the listing order provided to "users."

Like empowered desktop publishers, user-generated content was self-published by consumers in 1998 with their opinions and agendas (aka bloggers). The customer began sharing information, engaging brands in new ways, and creating value for other customers asking, "What's in it for me?"

With this development, media and technology shifted to inbound marketing—an inversion of the traditional with the consumer initiating engagement with the brands—at an incredible speed.

- 2003: Social media emerged to provide a community of different types of users.
- 2005: Search engines personalized results based on preferences.
- 2006: E-commerce expanded the marketplace.
- 2007: Mobile advanced with increased bandwidth for music and video.
- 2008: Apps extended the functionality of handheld communications.
- 2010: Email marketing reached 90 percent spam.
- 2011: Social sharing enabled customers to provide ratings and feed back.
- 2012: Geo-targeting placed ads based on customer location.
- 2013: Augmented reality supplemented the customer experience.
- 2014: Facebook "helps" users manage messages from liked pages by implementing an

algorithm selecting business page impressions, expands ad services and promotions to businesses.

Lessons from the Internet

- Technology continues developing faster than consumers can adopt it.
- The time needed to exploit a channel for marketing communication has reduced dramatically.
- Earned media is not paid media. Don't get the two confused.

Every type of medium before social media has followed the same path. First, there's innovation, then experimentation, adoption, commercialization, and finally, fragmentation.

As we introduce new technology into our ability to communicate, eventually it becomes less, and the message becomes more. Social media will continue to become less about the technology and more about the message. Like the technology that has come before, eventually the technology becomes transparent, and the user will only focus on communicating. When was the last time you thought about the technology that goes into connecting you with a person on your mobile phone or considered how an email shows up in your inbox?

No matter the channel(s) or technology, the task remains the same for business: getting enough of the right people to listen to your message and engage. Ultimately, you must make decisions about which technology to invest within, which communication channels to utilize, and how much is enough to reach your target markets.

Integrated Marketing Communications

Just as technology has evolved, so has the use of marketing communications. The once single-use advertisement is now the impetus for a print and outdoor campaign. Radio now supports the targeted television commercials seen during soap operas.

We learned we could increase the ROI of developing a message by applying the message to more media. We also learned we could strengthen marketing efforts by combining them, like braided wires into a cable, to support so much more than when used alone. These lessons learned are the basis for integrated marketing communications.

In 1989, the American Association of Advertising Agencies defined integrated marketing communications (IMC) as "an approach to achieving the objectives of a marketing campaign through a well-coordinated use of different promotional methods that are designed to reinforce each other.*" The short version is: All of your marketing looked like it came from the same place, it supported a common message, and all of it worked together.

The long version better explains integrated marketing communications as the development of marketing strategies and creative messages that utilize multiple marketing disciplines (like advertising, marketing, public relations, direct mail, pay-per-click, and social media). Selected for their individual contributions, each channel in the plan is coordinated with the other channels to achieve the goals of the overall plan. One shows the product, another tells them more, and another lets them try a sample for themselves. Instead of using a singular medium to tell the product story, IMC leverages the unique strengths of each communication channel to achieve a greater impact together than each channel could achieve alone.

A benefit of an IMC approach also allows one medium's weakness to be offset by another medium's strength. As the experienced have seen, a lot of things have to come together to make a marketing connection. Each of these marketing communications has inherent challenges in reaching the target audience—it's the "noise" that Shannon & Weaver demonstrated in their *Theory of Communications*. And no matter the message we send, there are successive steps, each dependent on the previous, that we must complete if the message is to even reach the receiver.

The Reality of Marketing

For decades, we've learned the best practices in marketing communications, yet there are —and always will be—inherent shortcomings in every type of communication. Just because you plan to communicate does not ensure the message will survive to reach the receiver, let alone the noise.

The name of your company has to communicate to your target market what you do yet distinguish you from the competition. Increase the geographic area, and it quickly becomes an overcrowded marketplace. If you need a domain name, get ready to revisit your second and third choices for a dot-com.

An email has to get through the corporate spam firewall and the personal junk filter, then survive the "delete" button during the recipient quick scan and still be compelling enough to get a click-through.

Direct mail has to be appealing enough to avoid getting tossed out during the mail sort above the garbage can. It has to be compelling enough to be opened, with an offer so strong the prospect can't help but respond (a formula so complex that Direct Marketing Association reports average response rates of under 4 percent)*.

A television commercial must run during a show your target audience watches (Morning 7 a.m. to 10 a.m. doesn't mean the "Today Show"). You have to execute this broadcast at the same time your target audience is watching the other commercials and the other screens (smartphone, tablet) that many viewers watch during commercials.

The radio advertisement has to be on the station at the same time your prospect is listening, sandwiched between the drive-time weather report and the latest pop single. It has to be memorable enough to continue the call-to-action when the prospect gets to a phone or computer.

The outdoor billboard has to be seen and thought memorable by your prospect, who is driving by at 65 mph, one hand on the wheel, the other dialing a cell phone or playing with the radio.

The print ad in the newspaper placed in the business section has to stop the prospects scanning the entire paper for something of interest—visual or textual. The message has to be strong enough to generate an action, or the ad was just an impression.

The printed brochure has to get into the hands of the prospect, get opened, survive the "once-over" flip-and-scan, then compel the prospect to retain the collateral until they dial the number, get online, or travel to a physical location.

The press release has to go out on a distribution channel to be picked up by the news source to which the editor subscribes as a source for the content prospects read in an issue the prospect reads.

The media must be developed on a platform that the greatest number of users utilize to access this type of media. Nothing is viewable by everyone.

You have to create an event that competes with other organizations doing the same thing at the same time for the same attendees even though you may not be a competitor. You are competing for that person's time, and there's only so much to go around.

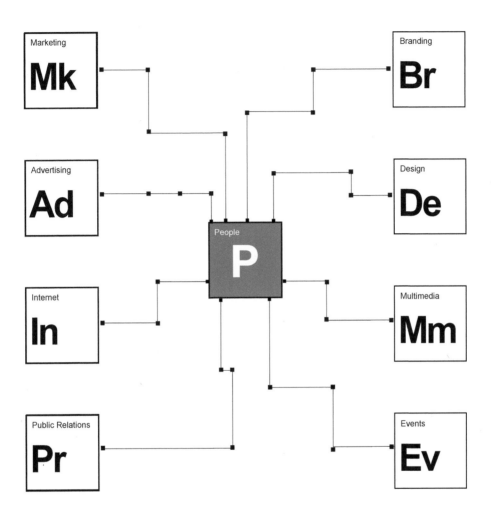

And let's not forget the Internet. Remember when the dot-coms came? The dream was that every business would build a website, and the customers would come. Well, they didn't—at least not as many as we wanted. So we "integrated" the web address into everything: business cards, radio spots, TV commercials, exterior signage, t-shirts—everything to try and lead the already/mildly interested prospects to the site.

Search engines were developed to help the consumer find the websites. This solution was great until marketers figured out how to game the system to get eyeballs (remember how many websites had white text on white pages to beat the formula trying to provide accurate results?).

Still not enough traffic.

So then marketers figured out a way to trick search engines into finding their sites based on user keyword search. When the search engines found out what marketers were doing, they changed their algorithms (the formulas their computers use to evaluate and prioritize search results). Instead of building better websites, marketers put money—lots of money—into companies that figured out what marketers couldn't: Search Engine Optimization (which some argue is more tricking the system). Marketing has tried different compensation models for SEO companies, like (eyeball) impressions, pay-per-click, and pay-per-transaction, and each has delivered varied results (depending on who you ask and what they were selling) —all of this to drive numbers into a poorly designed funnel ill-prepared to facilitate the sales process.

Appealing as it sounds, integrated marketing communications does require the marketer to understand each medium's requirements and its limitations, including the audience's ability to engage with the message. As my grandfather had demonstrated decades ago by watching television while listening to the radio and reading the paper, consumers integrate media by their preference and for their purpose. We can't tell them how to consume media, but we can prepare the media for their consumption.

Of course, proper planning prevents poor performance (5 more P's from Steven Osinski*), but there are no guarantees—at best you're making an educated guess at what will happen in the future. Just do your best to choose wisely from what you have learned. Focus on the consumer (Lauterborn), on what they want and need. Understand, what it costs them is more than just price. Make it convenient for them and consider the communication that best creates a dialog.

> *Growing up in advertising, I remember the ad guy lore that most prospects see 1 out of every 3 ads, and that in excess of 9 engagements are required to actually move the prospect toward the call to action: call, click, stop in, etc. High school math applied, it takes at least 27 instances of communication to get your prospects to the decision point: to buy or not to buy! Where are your 27 points of impression? Choose wisely. - kp*

Mass Communication Creates Mass Marketing Opportunities

History has shown advancements in technology dramatically impact communications. With social media enabling us to "join the conversation," our messages could be broadcast, aka "multiplied," by more people to reach other—to create new prospects. That's the real appeal in this mass communication. A business could be a source for what their customers wanted and needed by providing the right type of content. They could deliver when their customers wanted and needed it—well-placed right in the middle of where they are talking about it. Responses to a broadcasted message could a create conversation that is the basis for a social network, interaction, and, over time, engagement.

References

* Booms, Bernard H., & Bitner, Mary Jo (1981). *Marketing Strategies and Organization Structures for Service Firms. Marketing of Services.* American Marketing Association: 47–51.
* Borden, N. (1948). The Concept of the Marketing Mix. As retrieved: http://faculty.mu.edu.sa/public/uploads/1361463588.8451marketing%20mix5.pdf
* Chavira-Medford, M. (2011, June 6). Del Mar's Steven Osinski leaves corporate America for academia. *Del Mar Times.* Retrieved October 6, 2014, from: http://www.delmartimes.net/news/2011/jun/06/del-mars-steven-osinski-leaves-corporate-america/2/?#article-copy.
* Consumer-oriented movement [definition]. In *Wikipedia.* Retrieved from: http://en.wikipedia.org/wiki/Marketing_mix
* Integrated marketing communications (IMC) [definition]. From the *American Association of Advertising Agencies.* Retrieved from: http://www.businessdictionary.com/definition/integrated-marketing-communications-IMC.html.
* Lovelock, C., & Wirtz, J. (2011). *Services marketing: People, technology, strategy* (7th ed.). Boston: Prentice Hall.
* Lauterborn, B. (1990). *New Marketing Litany: Four Ps Passé: C-Words Take Over.* Advertising Age, 61 (41), 26. Crain Communications, Inc.
* McCarthy, Jerome E. (1960). *Basic Marketing: A Managerial Approach.* Homewood, IL: Richard D. Irwin
* Popovic, K. (2014). *Predicting the Digital Marketing Future: Learn from the Analog Past.* Retrieved from: http://www.onlinemarketinginstitute.org/blog/2014/03/predicting-the-digital-marketing-future-learn-from-the-analog-past/

* Shannon, C., & Weaver, W. (1964). *The Mathematical Theory of Communication.* Urbana: University of Illinois Press.
* Direct Marketing Association: 2012 Response Rate Report.
  http://www.marketingcharts.com/traditional/direct-mail-tops-email-for-response-rates-costs-per-lead-similar-22395/

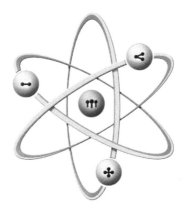

CHAPTER THREE

Defining Social Media

Definitions, by definition, are intended to add clarity to a word, a phrase or a concept. Introductory definitions serve as an education to the unknown, contributing to the formation of early thought, and subsequent definitions help facilitate discussion and potentially even create new thought.

At least, that's how it's supposed to work.

Like my colleagues, and perhaps you, I've been interested in how "social media" has been defined from its inception, and how it is being "defined" today as it continues to evolve. The once mystical is now familiar as social media have become a mainstay of popular personal and business communications. However, the accelerated rate of evolution keeps changing what it is, what it does, and how we all use it.

When I've asked people, "What is social media?" I more often get examples than a definition. Most will start off quickly with, "It's Facebook, YouTube, Twitter, you know…" then remember, "Google+, umm, LinkedIn…" They'll trail off as their eyes look to the ceiling in hopes of thinking of at least one or two more, and they never get to a definition. When people struggle with an answer, they revert to what they know, what they're comfortable with, so they start naming the sites they use. I find that speaks volumes on how difficult "social media" is to define.

As an early adopter of online communication (I'm talking AOL chat rooms in the early '90s), I know what I think it is. But much like defining "sex" on the playground in fourth grade, I'm very interested in what other people think it is too. I'll tell you now: the definitions are not all the same, and it depends on whom you ask—and that is a problem. If we can't all agree on what "it" is, how will we ever be able to use "it" together?

> *Before the social purists burst into a horde and light my effigy for insinuating the need for conformity in our online society, I'll clarify: That's NOT what I'm saying. All I AM saying is when defining "social media" consider—and compare—the sources of those definitions before you think you know where babies really come from.*

The Oxford Dictionary* defines social media as, "Websites and applications that enable users to create and share content or to participate in social networking." In other words, "Technology that helps people create and share content that facilitates communication."

Merriam-Webster* elaborated with: "Forms of electronic communication (as websites for social networking and micro-blogging) through which users create online communities to share information, ideas, personal messages, and other content (as videos)." This definition can also be restated as, "Technology that helps facilitate communication between people sharing content."

Looking to their digital equivalent, Wikipedia* (the free online encyclopedia) explains, "Social media is the social interaction among people in which they create, share or exchange information and ideas in virtual communities and networks." So even the encyclopedia that was developed via "crowdsourcing"—a volunteering crowd of contributors sharing content using technology toward a common project—infers social media is the communication between people sharing content using technology.

Academia provides examples from its ranks via Andreas Kaplan and Michael Haenlein*, professors of marketing at ESCP Europe Business School (Paris). They define social media as "a group of Internet-based applications that build on the ideological and technological foundations of Web 2.0, and that allow the creation and exchange of user-generated content." Again, in this definition, four keywords are referenced: technology, communication, content, and people.

Lastly, we look to business for its contribution in defining social media. Brian Solis, a digital strategist, bestselling author, and pioneer in social media marketing, wrote this definition in 2007* within his "Defining Social Media:" "Social media describes the online tools that people use to share content, profiles, opinions, insights, experiences, perspectives and media itself, thus facilitating conversations and interaction online between groups of people." Again, a definition that addresses technology, people, content, and communication.

Sure, that was in 2007, and social media has changed, and so have the definitions. In 2014*, Solis' definition evolved, just like social media itself, to reflect the changes we have experienced (whether we realized it or not). Solis said, "Social media is the democratization of information, transforming people from content readers into publishers. It is a shift from a broadcast mechanism, one-to-many to a many-to-many model, rooted in conversation between authors, people, and peers." Years later, even after the adoption by a majority of society and the evolution in social media, content, people, communication, and technology remain.

Although people have their reasons for communicating, a Pew Internet Research Report* found most Americans use social media to stay in touch with friends (64%) and family members (67%), with more women (72%) staying in touch with family than men (50%).

Reconnecting with friends with whom they have lost touch (50%) is second. Only 14% surveyed responded, "Connecting with others with shared hobbies or interests." The study noted, "There were no major differences on this question in terms of age, income, education, race/ethnicity, parental status or place of residence."

Admittedly, I'm leading to a concept, but I believe I do so well within business parameters, and responsibly within academic tolerances, to make an effort toward a common definition. Social media has been defined by many perspectives, and they all have something to do with people, technology, content, and communication. So, starting with those four words, we could define social media as: "People using content and technology to communicate with other people in their social network."

Types of Social Media

Another way to define social media is to examine its components—what is social media made of—and the reason for its existence—what do you do with it? By understanding there are different types of social media, we can better understand social media as a whole.

In version 4.0 of the Conversation Prism, Brian Solis has detailed 26 different types of social media* for our consideration. He explains, "Using the traditional definition, a prism separates white light into a spectrum of colors. The 'white light' in this case, is the focused stream of conversations that are often grouped, but not separated by voice, context, source, or outcome. We take this beam of dialog and blast it into a spectrum of discernible light, let's call it enlightenment, to see, hear, learn and adapt. We quite literally bring conversations to light. Used figuratively, it references the clarification or distortion afforded by a particular viewpoint…for example, 'We view conversations across the networks through the prism of our social dashboard.'"

1. Social Networks
2. Social Streams
3. Location
4. Quantified Self
5. Events
6. Livecasting
7. Enterprise
8. Content
9. Niche Working
10. Business
11. Influence
12. Music
13. Pictures
14. Blog / MicroBlog
15. Content / Documents
16. Wiki
17. Communicate
18. Discussion & Forums
19. Social Bookmarks
20. Social Curation
21. Q&A
22. Crowd Wisdom
23. Social Commerce
24. Service Networking
25. Reviews & Ratings
26. Social Marketplace

Solis' Conversation Prism has indeed dissected the "light" of social media to reveal unique facets. I, like many in our field, value the perspective he provides by addressing these nuances in distinguishing one from another. I do question, though, that those working to grasp the definition of social media may perceive social media as much more complicated than it needs to be.

I, like our colleagues, value the perspective his work provides us by addressing the nuances and subtleties, and in distinguishing one from another. Those working to grasp the definition, though, may view this as much more intricate than they are prepared to address.

In exploring a simpler approach, I began with Solis' detail and made list after list, working to reduce them to the most basic concepts. When I thought myself finished, I compared my list to other lists already published (everybody speaking to social media has a list—Google "types of social media"). I had email exchanges with some colleagues and late-night Google+ hangouts with others in a lively debate about why one goes on one list but not another.

In the end, I identified three big buckets that all of social media can generally fit into: Social Networking, Content Sharing and Collaboration.

1. Social Networking

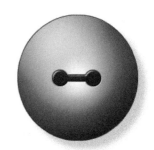

Social Networking sites like Facebook, LinkedIn or Twitter enable people to connect with other people. Whether it's for personal use or business, it's still a social networking service.

People use social networking to communicate: to share what they think (micro-blog) and to respond to others (comments). People share where they are (location) and what they're do-ing (events), providing additional context to their messages. Structured conversations, like a question and answer (Q&A), can provide a framework for communicating and can be scaled as necessary to accommodate the number of people and what they want to discuss (discussion and forums, crowd wisdom).

2. Content Sharing

Content Sharing sites help people share all of the different types of information and electronic media that can be shared using a social networking service or a website.

People can share text, documents, pictures, video, music, multimedia and the like. Content sharing sites also pro-vide the ability to construct content (blogs), to create an archive of content (social bookmarks, social curation), and to monitor its ongoing development (social streams). People can share their comments on the content at the source (ratings, reviews, discussion, forums) or at any place the content is shared.

Although people create most content in advance of sharing, some sites enable people to share their content while they are creating by broadcasting a real-time, synchronous stream (livecasting).

3. Collaboration

Social networking sites enable people to communicate, and content sharing sites enable people to share content.

Collaboration sites enable people to create a social network and to share content for a purpose. A group of people can collaborate on a small project (nicheworking) with a particular interest or with more people on a larger scale (wiki). People may collaborate to create social capital (influence) or for capital gain (social marketplace, social commerce), and a large group of people may collaborate on an enterprise level.

Do we have to make it any more complicated than that? And if we agree that's all social media is—another technology for people to communicate with other people—we can start applying what we know about communicating using technology and other media to communicate better.

The Business Opportunity

Throughout the history of communications, business has historically identified new technology that provides access to large numbers of people as opportunities for marketing messages. Social media is no different.

As we look to the future, reports indicate the average consumption of media by Americans will continue to increase to 15.5 hours per day per person by 2015*. According to The Institute for Communications Technology Management (CTM), mobile messages will increase to 28% of voice hours, video views will total over 11 hours a month (24% per year), and total hours on Facebook and YouTube will grow to 35.2 billion hours (a year over year growth rate of 28%).

Companies in the business-to-consumer (B2C) space are historically working to get in front of their consumers, and at the moment, social media provides two of the top-3 most trusted types of communications. Their consumers and their friends are the most trusted brand advocates they have. According to the 2013 Nielsen Trust in Advertising survey, 84% of online consumers trust the recommendations from their friends*. Accounting for friends of friends, that's a lot of potential new customers.

Companies that market their services to other companies are in the Business-to-Business (B2B) category. Although B2B and B2C are often treated differently, I maintain they are still people who are trying to communicate with people. Sure, the job title "Mom" is different than "CEO," but they're both online and accessible. They are both online talking about what you want them to talk about, and in most cases, you are invited to "join the conversation" just as social media has always promoted. The content of B2B messages is going to be a little different than B2C, but the process of communication is the same.

The same goes for businesses categorized as non-profit and not-for-profit organizations—foundations, charities, or political action committees. Each has found social media appealing for many of the same reasons: reaching people, collecting recommendations from others, and leveraging public opinion.

Creating Social Capital

Every person using social media starts with some information about themselves: You create a username, add an icon, a picture, a quote, a birthday, a family photo, an update in your professional life, or the status of your relationship. You present some information, some type of content that attracts others and facilitates interaction between two people.

A "like" on Facebook, a "favorite" on Twitter, a +1 on Google+—each social network has a metaphor for acknowledgment and positive feedback on the content and activity without actually having to type, "Hey, I like that." It is this type of activity, over time, which builds awareness and creates a relationship between people in social media. Repeated interactions within their network leads people to learn more about each other, and the generating of lists of the others they interact with frequently—friends, followers, connections—works with technology of the social networking service to facilitate more interaction.

The greater the perceived value of the interaction, the greater the value of the connection, which leads to the creation of social capital, a term borrowed from sociology to describe the perceived value placed on the sometimes intangible relationship of a social network.

French sociologist Pierre Bourdieu defined social capital as, "The aggregate of the actual or potential resources which are linked to possession of a durable network of more or less institutionalized relationships of mutual acquaintance and recognition." Much like the "old boys network" of days gone by or the "who you know" in business, social capital can be exchanged for something of value. In his "Forms of Capital" (1986), Bourdieu writes:

It is what makes the games of society—not least, the economic game—something other than simple games of chance offering at every moment the possibility of a miracle. Roulette, which holds out the opportunity of winning a lot of money in a short space of time, and therefore of changing one's social status quasi-instantaneously, and in which the winning of the previous spin of the wheel can be staked and lost at every new spin, gives a fairly accurate image of this imaginary universe of perfect competition or perfect equality of opportunity, a world without inertia, without accumulation, without heredity or acquired properties, in which every moment is perfectly independent of the previous one, every soldier has a marshal's baton in his knapsack, and every prize can be attained, instantaneously, by everyone, so that at each moment anyone can become anything. Capital, which, in its objectified or embodied forms, takes time to accumulate and which, as a potential capacity to produce profits and to reproduce itself in identical or expanded form, contains a tendency to persist in its being, is a force inscribed in the objectivity of things so that everything is not equally possible or impossible. And the structure of the distribution of the different types and subtypes of capital at a given moment in time represents the immanent structure of the social world, i.e., the set of constraints, inscribed in the very reality of that world, which govern its functioning in a durable way, determining the chances of success for practices.

Nan Lin, a professor of sociology of the Trinity College at Duke University, was much more concise but just as to-the-point in his definition of social capital, calling it an "Investment in social relations with expected returns in the marketplace." Lin's research specific to social networks and social capital explains the importance of using social connections and social relations in achieving goals. "Social capital, or resources accessed through such connections and relations, is critical (along with human capital, or what a person or organization actually possesses) in achieving goals for individuals, social groups, organizations, and communities." Lin states, "It is 'who you know', as well as 'what you know' that makes a difference in life and society."

The People Using Social Media

To utilize a social networking service, each person must create a user profile—it's what distinguishes you from another person using the same service. Like a telephone number or a mailing address, a user profile serves as a personal representation and a point of contact. A username, an avatar, a profile or a page— each represents you to others using the same service.

The service (usually) facilitates the introduction to other users because that's the business they are in – creating a social network for each user. The service also (usually) enables users to identify other users already known to them from school, work, or existing personal relationships with the click of a button or an input of your username and password to access known contacts in your email account.

Identifying and connecting with others is the start of a social network, and a collection of all the users is an online community. The difference between the two is that the social network is user-centric, while an online community is group-centric. More simply, one is about the person and the other is about the group.

Most social networking services are Internet-based and include instant messaging, email or publishing capabilities to communicate. They enable users to initiate a series of activities, like sharing ideas, interests, events, pictures, video, audio, and links to other content from other users from within and across other Internet services using hyperlinks (the basis for the World Wide Web). They also provide users the ability to respond to the message and reply with synchronous and asynchronous responses. Synchronous responses, meaning at the same time, can be represented as a chat window or as real-time updates. Asynchronous responses, meaning not at the same time, can be emails or messages that receive a reply at a later date. The message is sent from one user to another, and the receiver can respond, but it's the time in between that differentiates synchronous and asynchronous: They're both still communication.

In 2013, the US Census reported that the U.S. population is 317.3 million people, give or take*. According to a 2014 Pew Research Internet Project report, 87% of all Americans are online —on the Internet. Of those 276,051,000 people, some 74% of online adults (204,277,740) are now using a social networking site of some kind.* It also means that 113,022,260 are not.

> *87% of American adults now use the Internet. We see near-saturation usage among those living in households earning $75,000 or more (99%), young adults ages 18-29 (97%), and those with college (97%). Fully 68% of adults connect to the Internet with mobile devices like smartphones or tablet computers. The adoption of related technologies has also been extraordinary: Over the course of Pew Research Center polling, adult ownership of cell phones has risen from 53% in their first survey in 2000 to 90% now. Ownership of smartphones has grown from 35% when they first asked in 2011 to 58% now.*

According to the Pew Social Networking Fact Sheet, 72% of all men and 76% of all women on the Internet are social media users. The report measured ages 18-65+ and showed of the 18-29 year olds online, 89% were users, followed by 30-49 year olds (82%), 50-64 year olds

(65%) and users 65 and older (49%). As the age group grew older, the percentage of social media users decreased. Now that doesn't mean older people aren't using social media to communicate, it just means there are more young people using social media.

People of all education levels are using social media, some a little more than others. College students who did not complete their degree (78%) are more likely to use social media than those who completed college (73%)—perhaps they have more free time looking online for employment. Seventy-two percent of high school students on the Internet—degree or no degree—are using social media.

Socioeconomic reports provide similar numbers as education. There exists a slight variance between brackets, but earnings between brackets had little to do with using social media (70-79%), and still roughly three of every four people online were using social media.

The number of users changes daily, depending on whom you ask and what specifically you ask: How many users? Total users or active users? Define an active user or an inactive user. That being said, Pew reports: 71% of online adults use Facebook, 19% use Twitter, 17% use Instagram, 21% use Pinterest, 22% use LinkedIn.

The People Using Social Media

Facebook	Twitter	Instagram	Pinterest	LinkedIn
Fb 71%	**Tw** 19%	**In** 17%	**Pi** 21%	**Li** 22%

Missing from the report, but perhaps not as obvious, is Google+ (2011) and the veteran MySpace (circa 2003). Check the obituaries for their current status. You could list others as well, but the intent at this time is to gain a general understanding of the types of social media and the people who are using social media.

Although these statistics will most likely shift one way or another as this book is being published, these provide a base impression of the audience, their activity, and a benchmark for future and more current statistics.

Social Media Is Media

Like other media, "social" has multiple channels to connect with people that match demographic and psychographic profiles. Like other media, we can research social media in advance to target an audience based on the same criteria we use for selecting traditional media, including:

- Demographics: The quantitative information about users, like age, gender, education, income, geographic location.
- Psychographics: The qualitative information about users, like why they use social media, why they do what they do online.
- Reach: The number of unique people that view a message.
- Frequency: How often a message is presented to a target audience.
- Impressions: How many times a message is displayed.
- CPM: The average cost incurred to present a message to 1,000 people.
- ROI: The return on investment.

As we work toward a common understanding of social media, I suggest if we agree that social media is another type of media, then we could apply what we already know about using technology and content to communicate with target audiences—which is a lot—to communicating with those on social media.

A Broader Understanding

Throughout this chapter, I have worked to provide a broader understanding of social media by examining the multiple perspectives and influences we all encounter. In deconstructing definitions, I believe we have identified the essence of social media—people, content, technology, and communication. We've developed a foundation of understanding social media as "People using content and technology to communicate with other people in their social network."

The numbers further support this definition. According to Data Never Sleeps*, every minute of every day on social media:

- Google receives over 2,000,000 search queries
- Facebook users share 684,478 pieces of content
- Twitter users send over 100,000 tweets
- Brands and organizations on Facebook receive 34,7222 "likes"
- Tumblr blog owners publish 27,778 new posts
- Instagram users share 3,600 new photos

- Flickr users add 3,125 new photos
- FourSquare users perform 2,083 check-ins
- WordPress users publish 347 new blog posts

People are using social media to communicate. By examining the spectrum of social media in Solis' Conversation Prism, we can see the extent to which social media has already fragmented into thousands of channels. By learning from history, we can expect this to continue. Knowing this will provide context as you develop your approach.

A business opportunity exists within this media channel that does make it unique from others: the opportunity to engage, to generate a conversation with the people using your product and services or that support your cause. By matching your target demographics to those of social media networking services you can locate an audience, understand the content that attracts your prospects and identify opportunities for engagement. Remember, people love to buy but hate being sold. Our job in business is to facilitate the sales process. Like Lauterborn suggested, the ability to provide the consumer what they want, when they need it, is important.

Therein lies the opportunity in social media.

References

* Bourdieu, P. (1986). The Forms of Capital. *Handbook of Theory and Research for the Sociology of Education*, 241-258.
* Domo. Data Never Sleeps. Retrieved from: http://www.domo.com/learn/infographic-data-never-sleeps/
* Institute for Communication Technology Management (CTM) at the USC Marshall School of Business and CTM Visiting Researcher Short, E. James., (2013). Consumption of Media in the US: The U.S. consumption of media is the topic of "How Much Media? 2013 Report on American Consumers. Retrieved from: http://www.marshall.usc.edu/news/releases/2013/usc-ctm-releases-report-americans-media-consumption
* Kaplan, A., & Haenlein, M. (n.d.). Users of the world, unite! The challenges and opportunities of Social Media. *Business Horizons*, 59-68.
* Lin, N. (2002). Social Capital: A Theory of Social Structure and Action. Retrieved from: http://www.cambridge.org/us/academic/subjects/sociology/social-theory/social-capital-theory-social-structure-and-action

* Nielsen: 2013 Nielsen Trust in Advertising survey Smith, A. (2011). Why Americans Use Social Media. Retrieved from: http://www.pewinternet.org/2011/11/15/why-americans-use-social-media/

* Social Media [Def. 1]. Oxford Dictionaries. Retrieved September 30, 2014, from http://www.oxforddictionaries.com/us/definition/american_english/social-media

* Social Media [Def. 1]. Merriam-Webster Online. In Merriam-Webster. Retrieved September 30, 2014, from http://www.merriam-webster.com/dictionary/social%20media.

* Social Media Marketing. (n.d.). In Wikipedia. Retrieved October 16, 2014 from: http://en.wikipedia.org/wiki/Social_media_marketing

* Social Networking Fact Sheet. (2013, December 27). Retrieved October 20, 2014, from http://www.pewinternet.org/fact-sheets/social-networkingfact-sheet/

* Solis, B. (2007). Defining Social Media. Retrieved from: http://www.briansolis.com/2007/06/defining-social-media/

* Solis, B. (2010). 10 Quotes on The Future of Business. Retrieved from: http://www.briansolis.com/category/articles/new-communications/

* Solis, B., & JESS3. The Conversation Prism. Retrieved from: http://upload.wikimedia.org/wikipedia/commons/7/7c/Conversationprism.jpeg

* U.S. Census Bureau. (2013). U.S Population 2013. Retrieved from: http://www.census.gov/popest/data/national/asrh/2013/index.html

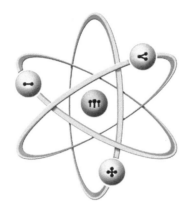

CHAPTER FOUR

7 Reasons You Should Not Use Social Media For Your Business

There are thousands of social media authors, experts, consultants, mavens, and gurus. Some of them are self-proclaimed, preaching on top of a soapbox about the wow and now of social media. Others have earned the right to preach and share their encouraging messages, but too often it's only the "good word" of social media. They're all preaching—they need to fill their donation plate—and they're all making money when you buy into social media. By the way, thank you for purchasing my book on social media.

It also appears there is no shortage of books, articles and white papers showcasing the success stories of businesses using social media to meet their goals. Every story has a happy ending, and someone gets something you wish you had in the end. Like statistics, there are more than enough success stories for you to reference (p161) to make your case to choose social media. But what most will not share with you is the cold hard truth about social media.

One of my mentors has been Keith Hall, the CEO of Leadership Advantage, former director of medical training for GlaxoSmithKline, and an all-around great guy. Keith and I worked together for years, and as our personal friendship developed, Keith would share his wisdom as my "Dutch Uncle." Very to-the-point and for my own good, he would tell me all the things I didn't want to hear but needed to know. At times, I didn't want to hear anything other than that I was right—I had an idea in my mind—but in the end, his insight was on point and it served me well. So, for that same purpose (for your own good, with your best interest in mind), I'm going to tell you NOT to use social media for your business.

Not what you were expecting? Neither is social media.

Reason #1: Your Audience Isn't There

Social media is current and trending as a communications channel, but that doesn't guarantee the people you are trying to reach are there. Pew (2013) reports 87% of Americans are online which means 13% are not. Of those 87% online, 26% don't use social media*. Depending on your audience demographics and psychographics, there's a good chance they're not there.

A 2014 Gallup survey* of 18,000 U.S. consumers report that people primarily use social media to be social. Ninety-four percent of social media users do so to connect with friends and family, 29% to follow trends, find information and product reviews and 20% to add their comments to product reviews.

As far as the influence they have on purchasing decisions: 62% have no influence at all, 30%

have some (influencers), and only 5% have a great deal of influence (influencers) on making a purchase. Statistically, people didn't join social media for the business. One in three will talk about products and services, but only one in 20 buys.

Before you invest any time in developing a social media presence be sure your audience is using social media, and you know where they are. The Internet is a big place and just because Facebook is your favorite social networking service doesn't necessarily make it the best starting place for your business.

Reason #2: Social Media Doesn't Work for Every Business

Despite popular opinion, social media marketing does not work for every business. And no matter how much using social media to communicate makes sense to you, it has to make sense to your audience or it just won't work.

Financial advisors, for instance, have regulatory organizations that restrict the information they can share and the comments they make on that information. Doctors have (HIPAA) restrictions prohibiting what they can say about patients to protect patient privacy, and lawyers have a code of ethics and are bound by state and federal laws. Pharmaceutical companies are just as heavily regulated, and penalties—financial and legal—come quickly for breaking the rules.

You have to be in an industry that uses social media to communicate, and you have to use the right type of social media.

Retail fashion is a good business for social media engagement; it's largely women (ages 13–55) sharing content (mostly pictures and links to articles) and discussing what they like and what they don't. Since it's photo and news driven, many options are available, such as Facebook, Pinterest, Instagram, and Tumblr. Those familiar with social media can probably recall seeing a fashion brand on social media for one thing or another.

A bad business for social media engagement is medical marijuana. Although legal in many states, it's still illegal according to federal regulations. Although dispensaries and collectives can share pictures and information, customers are often reluctant to like a page on Facebook, follow on Twitter, or subscribe on YouTube to include them in their social network for fear of reflecting on them personally or professionally. As we saw for one of our clients, a lot of customers supported the business but didn't want their family or employers to know they use marijuana (for whatever reason), so building an audience was difficult.

Social media has to work for your business with your audience. If you can't communicate with the people and share information in a public space, it doesn't make sense for your business to use social media.

Reason #3: There Are Easier Ways to Get in Front of Your Audience

One of the biggest attractions to social media for businesses is the potential audience, but one of the biggest myths is that you can get one.

"Social media is not the powerful and persuasive marketing force many companies hoped they would be," concludes Gallup Inc. U.S. companies spent $5.1 billion on social-media advertising in 2013, but Gallup says "consumers are highly adept at tuning out brand-related Facebook and Twitter content."*

According to Beevolve (2014), the average Twitter user has less than 50 followers*, while the average Top 100 Companies in America (as reported in *Forbes**) has 7,789. Even if you can perform as well as one of the Top 100 Companies in America you cannot expect to gain more than 8,000 followers. And that's followers, not customers or purchases. To build this mean audience, it took the average Top 100 Company:

- 3 tweets per day, 2 of them about the brand
- 17,503 total tweets
- 9,045 brand tweets excluding @replies and retweets.
- Tweets including 11,312 links, 10,473 hashtags
- Average monthly engagement: 671

Is all this work in social media really a better idea than buying print advertisements or cable television or local radio? Print still delivers, as do radio, outdoor, and television. There are other proven ways to reach your audience—places where they already are and using technologies they already use—even the U.S. postal service.

If you do include social media in your communications plan, utilize it as part of an integrated marketing plan. Connect social media with advertisements in print, promotions on television, sales on radio, events on billboards and targeted digital campaigns online.

Reason #4: You Don't "Get It"

I see business after business create a profile or a page, upload a logo and some pictures, then plan to figure out what they're going to do with social media. Then … nothing. While it sits idly, it acts as a giant billboard telling people you don't know how to use social media for business, and you don't have a plan.

Social media isn't a sales call; it's a help call. Remember Lauterborn: It's not your marketing department pushing product, it's the people from the showroom floor introducing visitors to new information and answering questions—they're helping, not selling.

Despite all the definitions and metaphors, sometimes people just don't "get" social media—and that's okay, just don't them put in charge of the decision making or execution. We each have a role on the team, and everyone can't play quarterback (obligatory sports reference). If you don't understand why somebody you don't know wants to be your friend or why someone you don't know "likes" your page, then social media is not for you.

Reason #5: Social Media Is Not Free

Social is the Ikea® of media. It's the DIY (do-it-yourself) of communications. You have to pick something you think matches the current setting, in a size you think is going to fit, that serves the purpose for which it's selected. The out-of-the-box cost is cheaper than other choices, but it's not free. You have to pull it down from the shelf. You have to wheel it down the aisle. You have to strap it to your car, get it home safe, then up two flights of stairs. When you finally get it home you have to try and build it with tools you're not sure how to use, with directions that just don't make sense. What seemed like such a value can cost so much more in the end.

To use social media, you need a computer, a tablet, or a smartphone. You need access to the Internet. You need email to create accounts, pictures you can legally share, and lots of ideas of things to say to people you don't know who you may or may not find interesting, funny, or smart.

The internal costs of staff and resources to develop social profiles, create content, and build engagement comes from somebody's budget. It takes work over time to develop an audience on social media, and if you're not going to do the work, then you'll be paying someone to do it for you. How many hours would it take to develop 17,503 messages—and whose hours would they be? I'll caution entrepreneurs and the small business owners now not to discount sweat equity. Keep in mind, you could also invest the hours you spend for social media in other aspects of your business.

To begin, you'll need to identify people you know on the same social networking service and attract them to your profile to establish a common relationship, creating a friend, follower or subscriber. You will do this continually to build an audience and you will have to figure out how to keep them engaged over time. Sure, there are free, quality resources online with experienced instructors (yours truly included). They can teach you how to do all of this, like I do, but you'll have to find time in your schedule to learn not only what you need to know now, but what you'll need to learn more about when there is something new or a change in how things work. This situation happens quite a lot, often without notice.

Even if you did have the time to learn, you don't have the time it takes to be successful.

According to *Forbes**, nearly 50% of small businesses have increased the amount of time they invest in social media marketing. Nearly 55% are using social media mainstays, like Facebook and Twitter, as "the primary toolkit for either acquiring new customers [or] generating sales leads." Despite their dedication, more than 60% of small business owners report "no return on investment from their engagement online. None."

Social media is a lot of things, but it's not free, it's not a magic bullet and it isn't going to fix a bad business.

Reason #6: You Can't Find the ROI

My father taught me something was either a cost or an investment. A cost is something you spend money on and then it's gone. You have nothing to show for it. An investment is money you spend, and you get something in return. Before you run to social media, ask yourself, "What will have to happen on social media for my business to realize a return on investment?"

In the old days (2007), all businesses had to do was get users to "like" their fan page to create a 24/7 opt-in marketing channel. Pages would post a message, and every fan would see the message, no matter how many fans or how many times they would post. The quid pro quo was, "We'll give you what you want, and you'll put up with us working some marketing into the feed." The deal seemed to be working out for businesses and their fans, but not for Facebook.

Even after all the hours and dollars business has invested in Facebook (and other social media following suit), many of us who work professionally in social media see the (pending) death of earned media: The potential exposure you could get in front of a person after they "liked" your page. Now, paid media is the norm for business on many social networking sites —fans or not. It's pay-to-play.

On Facebook, businesses can no longer market at will. According to a report from Ogilvy via *AdAge* (2014), fan page organic reach is crashing* as Facebook "helps" determine how much of which fan page posts should make it to each userF. Best estimates are down to 1 to 2% of the fans already earned*. "Increasingly Facebook is saying that you should assume a day will come when the organic reach is zero." The justification from Facebook has been "there's only so much room in the newsfeed of our users" for business-related items—and it's true (to Facebook's advantage). If Facebook presented every post from a fan page that a user liked, how often would they see a post from their friends? Just like every other type of media, social media has a capacity, and once the capacity is reached the once commodity space becomes a premium space. Today, if you want to cut the line at the social club, you better be ready to tip the guy at the door.

To justify the pending investments in time, resources, and services, you have to find the ROI. A business must have measurable goals and the data that proves social media was worth it. A business looks to sales first, yet they are the hardest deliverable to create. What is your metric for success? How long will it take to realize the return? What are you going to tell your boss when he asks, "How are we doing?"

If you can't tell somebody where your business will find the ROI, then you should not use social media for your business.

Reason #7: Shit Happens

There are issues unique to social media that most businesses never consider when using social media—until after the fact or until it's too late. Even with the best of plans, what happens when something goes wrong? Something, on some scale, always goes wrong—then what? You find yourself on the front of something with a headline that isn't flattering. You turn into the butt of a joke, and suddenly, there are a lot of questions about "How did this happen?" and "Who is to blame?"

Here are some lessons to learn and scenarios to run through as you consider using social media to communicate with your audience.

Nothing ever disappears. You may have a less-than-stellar moment then delete something you did, but someone may have captured a copy, and it could resurface at any time. Usually, it'll pop up when you don't want it to (Murphy's Law). Years after a Twitter-based "sexting" scandal the pictures of Congressman Anthony Weiner still display in any Google search.

News travels fast. No pressure, but one mistake, one misstep, one something from the past that just got leaked, and everyone will know. The imperfect misstep can bring everything you've worked so hard to build crashing down around you (search June Shannon from TLC's *Honey Boo-Boo*). No matter the outcome, people usually remember the mistake.

Public humiliation. Start with the little things, like a misspelling or referring to something incorrectly, and somebody notices. Post something you think is cute or smart, but it turns out it's insensitive or something you didn't realize (like the red splattered Kent State sweatshirt sold by Urban Outfitters). The public humiliation and embarrassment of not being one of the cool kids was hard enough in high school, now you want to do THIS in front of your customers. Good luck, but don't mess up.

Losing the balance between Personal and Professional. Your business is your professional side, but you have your personal opinions, too. Sharing them can be catastrophic, especially with those who oppose your view and perspective (search Paula Deen). You have to understand where the line is, and you have to know if you can cross it with prospects, customers, employees, partners, clients, government, media, etc.

When private goes public. Just because you can manage yourself on social media doesn't mean everyone can. The co-worker who doesn't know that "no means no," the contract that goes bad, the disgruntled employee who wants to make a final statement—all stories of when social goes bad. When unhappy customers start using #fail in their messages about your company how will you explain to other customers unaware of any issues?

Mistaken identity. Starting with "John Smith," how many times do you think people misidentify someone on the Internet? How easy is it to misspell an unfamiliar name or a company username, only to find something you did not expect to find? For the less experienced, I'll warn you: It's easier than finding the right person. People aren't the only ones who can be impacted by mistaken identity. When handling social media for the popular exercise phenomenon, Shake Weight, we identified 163 fraudulent Facebook pages using the client's logo and photos and 43 fake Twitter accounts (which took months to address).

Getting hijacked. Creating an attention-getting social media campaign is great until it gets so much attention it gets hijacked. The name of your campaign or the #hashtag used to distinguish itself from other content becomes a joke, and all your good work gets polluted. Worse is hijacking a trending hashtag and getting called out on it publicly (search "hashtags gone wrong").

A violation of trust. In business, we deal with a lot of secrets and proprietary information. At the very least, there are things you want to keep private. With everything digital and moving so fast, the wrong attachment in an email or the wrong click of a button could share information you did not intend to share. Even the military is looking at the vulnerability of social media. Those we trust in positions of power and access are also access points to critical information. How many people at your company do you think are the type who would share it all on a bad exit?

Bad timing. With social media, you just can't "set it and forget it." The popularity of social media applications scheduling social media posts for later dates does provide some efficiency, but it also removes you from what is going on. An unexpected hurricane can not only wreak havoc on a community you serve, but an automated message about the weather may be ill received in its wake. Weekend messages scheduled on a Friday may not be appreciated during a service outage over the weekend among customers who are using the same channel to complain about service. This collision could leave more than just nasty messages in your inbox.

You don't have a plan. The line, "Fail to plan, plan to fail" is concise but does not even start to address what can go wrong with social media. Most businesses don't understand they need policies and guidelines in place to help avoid situations and a crisis-management protocol in place before something goes south. Develop a social media strategy in advance, THEN create your social media policy. Create a communications plan that will direct how you utilize these assets to meet your goals and know how you'll manage your success.

A Fair and Balanced Report

I know I've presented social media in a hard light, and I've provided numerous reasons—based on my knowledge and experiences—not to use social media. Perhaps this is a bit odd for a book about how to use social media to create engagement, but not from your Dutch uncle who has your best interest at heart.

Too often, media, especially social media, share stories of success that are too good to believe: shortcuts to 1,000 fans, tips to getting 10,000 followers, or "how to make a viral video" that gets 100,000 views. The likelihood of you achieving the same success reported in these stories is about as likely as you hitting the lottery. Good luck.

Now that doesn't mean you can't have success using social media to create engagement. As you move forward now in deciding if and how to use social media, you do so with eyes wide open.

References

- Pew Internet Research Project: Social Media Report http://www.pewinternet.org/2013/12/30/social-media-update-2013/
- Gallup Survey, *Wall Street Journal:* http://online.wsj.com/articles/companies-alter-social-media-strategies-1403499658
- Casserly, Meghan. Why Small Businesses Are Losing on Social Media. (2013). *Forbes.* Retrieved from: http://www.forbes.com/sites/meghancasserly/2013/04/17/why-small-businesses-are-losing-on-social-media/
- Urso, Tara. Y*our Facebook Page's Organic Reach Is About to Plummet.* (2014). Retrieved from: http://www.socialmediatoday.com/content/your-facebook-pages-organic-reach-about-plummet
- *AdAge* / Ogilvy says Facebook plummeting, eventually zero: http://adage.com/article/digital/brands-organic-facebook-reach-crashed-october/292004/
- Lee, Jessica. *How Do You Stack Up Against Top Brands on Twitter?* [Study], (2014). Retrieved from: http://searchenginewatch.com/arti cle/2324540/How-Do-You-Stack-Up-Against-Top-Brands-on-Twitter- Study
- Elder, Jeff. (2014). *Social Media Fail to Live Up to Early Marketing Hype Companies Refine Strategies to Stress Quality Over Quantity of Fans.* Retrieved from: http://online.wsj.com/articles/companies-alter-social- media-strategies-1403499658

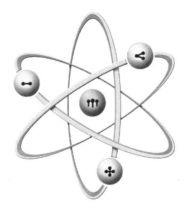

CHAPTER FIVE

The Satellite Marketing Process

"A specific goal has a much greater chance of being accomplished than a general goal."

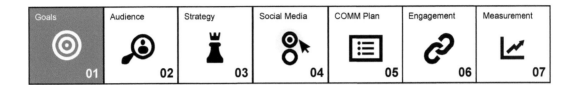

STEP 1

Identifying Goals

Whether it's improving customer service or generating an increase in leads, there has to be a reason you're looking to social media for your business.

Whenever I think of goals, I remember a bumper sticker that read, "If you don't know where you're going, how will you know when you get there?" This sticker was placed next to a bunch of other stickers on a car bumper whose make I can't even remember, but the message always stuck with me.

Author Simon Sinek's* book, *Start With Why,* is, indeed, a good place to start when we look to social media for business. In it, Sinek helps us "identify the purpose, cause, or belief that inspires you to do what you do." Admittedly, the book is about getting to the "why" of a brand proposition or to the "why" of a tactic. Still, many of the ideas he presents have their application in individual strategies you're developing to support your brand. So, tell me: Why social?

What do you hope to accomplish using social media? Why can't other media be used to do the same? And how will you know when you have accomplished what you set out to achieve? These are the types of questions that have to get answered before any others. If you don't answer these questions now, you will not know where you are going, and you will not know how to get there or when (hopefully) you've arrived.

To be fair, I've had clients return the question, asking, "It depends on what we can do with social media, doesn't it?" We've talked about the functionality of social media earlier in the book but not as much about the "why" of it. Some clients have little personal experience and aren't aware of the possibilities, so asking those clients to set goals by themselves puts them at a bit of a disadvantage. Sure, they probably know the basics, but they don't know all the obvious or potential applications. Remember that social media is media, and what we can do with one medium we can generally do with the others.*

*I know there will be immediate exceptions, but suspend your sense of disbelief and start with the same expectations you would have with other media and we'll get through the process together. The more you see what is being done, the more you'll see opportunities to apply these strategies to your business. - kp

Most often, there is more than one reason. Raising brand awareness, introducing a new product, fostering ongoing relationships with your customers, attracting new customers, introducing a new brand identity: Why? Think of the good reasons you're going to invest in social media—the "why," as well as the "what," "where" and "how" you're going to get a return on investment (ROI).

> *Remember: pennies make dollars. The more things you have contributed to your ROI, the greater the total return. Learning how to measure the ROI will come later, but know now, while you're setting goals, that at some point someone is going to ask you, "How is our social media going?" and you're going to want to tell them, "Very well, thank you." - kp*

Start with, "What do I think I/we can accomplish using social media for our business?" Write it down. Seriously. If you can't write it down and mold it to a point where it looks like it makes sense, you probably can't communicate it when you have to sell this idea to your colleagues, your boss, or your customers.

I'll give you an example. My reason for using social media for my business is: I'm investing in social media to create a contemporary perception of my brand, to increase the reach of my message, and to generate new customers.

It's nothing complicated, it's nothing extraordinary and it's easy to understand. It's the same as many businesses using social media, and it would be difficult for anyone to argue these weren't realistic and achievable.

Based on my statement for using social media, I have three distinct goals to achieve:

1. Create social media profiles for my business that perpetuate my existing branding
2. Build my social network from the users of select social media sites
3. Use the social network to generate leads that turn into clients

Each of the goals is clear in its direction, and each is measurable, albeit in different units of measurement.

Pass/Fail

Goal No. 1 is either done or it isn't, like a to-do. I can identify when a social media profile is complete: All the fields are completed, and I have some content in all the places where content goes. I can confirm that it has maintained established s for my company branding: The logo is in place, sized appropriately, and the current tagline is included. Using these guidelines, when I meet the criteria, I will have reached this goal.

Quantitative

Goal No. 2 measures numbers. Cumulatively, I can count and organize my social media network. The audience of each social media profile is quantifiable—the system tells me how many friends, followers, connections, subscribers, et al. that I have. It will tell me their names, where they are located, their job titles, and other data. I even can get peripheral data, such as how many connections my connections have (LinkedIn) or how many people my post reached (Facebook).

We can also measure the numerical activity on social media like number of posts, re-tweets, recommendations, reviews, links—more data. Each social media site provides some type of quantitative information to users about their profiles and pages (likes, fans, followers, posts, comments, etc.)—you just have to look for the data. Third-party tools and services can access profiles to interconnect social media (using API's and Open Source) to show cumulative data across multiple platforms then generate reports (so you don't have to) for a complete social media network.

Qualitative

Goal No. 3 is qualitative. Some people are more valuable to you in reaching your goals than others depending on who they are, what they do, and what type of relationship you can generate with them. The types of people in a social network are a critical yet frequently overlooked part of the ROI equation. When you don't account for the value of a connection, you're not providing an accurate measurement of your success.

In reaching my last goal—using the social network to generate leads that turn into clients—an audience of Decision Makers (CEOs, CMOs, VPs) is more likely to generate the clients I want than an audience of Influencers (Directors, Managers) or Referrals (Staff, Consultants). Decision Makers are motivated to improve the status of the company or to increase sales, and they have both the budget and the authority to hire a company that can provide services to do so. Influencers bring ideas to the table but don't have the authority to engage my company. Referrals can introduce me to an Influencer or Decision Maker, but the distance to authority and from budget reduces their value in my evaluation of their contribution toward my goals (nothing personal).

Rubric

By using a simple rubric—a measurement tool that rates my connections —I can generate a quantitative value for the quality of my connections. Rubrics are used by educators to apply consistent criteria for grading assignments and can be appropriately applied to the evaluation of a social network.

Each connection is a unique element that comprises my social network. Being able to identify them, understand their characteristics and measure their individual weights gives you a very different understanding of what you have achieved.

In this Social Network Evaluation Rubric, I have identified three types of people: a Referral, an Influencer and a Decision Maker. It's a simple progression of the types of people we meet in business with one other notation: whether or not they have a budget (i.e., the money to hire my company). I considered each of these people and distributed the weight accordingly— Decision Makers with Budget were the most valuable because they can sign a contract and cut a check.

Social Network Evaluation Rubric

Referral	Influencer	Influencer +Budget	Decision Maker	Decison Maker +Budget
Re 01	**In** 03	**In**^{B} 05	**Dm** 07	**Dm**^{B} 10

- Connection is a referral within the company: 1 pt
- Connection is an influencer within the company: 3 pts
- Connection is an influencer within the company and has a budget: 5 pts
- Connection is a decision maker within the company: 7 pts
- Connection is a decision maker within the company and has a budget: 10 pts

Using this metric, I can review each connection and assign points based on what I know about them today. Based on my 4,898 LinkedIn connections, my social network is worth 32,816 points, and my average connection is a 6.2 (at least an Influencer with their company). I can also measure the sales that have come from my connections to ultimately answer the questions I started with: Why am I looking to social media? What do I hope to accomplish? And how will I know when I have accomplished my goal(s)?

Term

There needs to be a term to every period of measurement to gauge accurate measurement. You don't just want to know the score, you want to know if you won the game. When are you going to start measuring? How frequently and for how long will you measure your social media progress?

The term will impact the perception of your information. Reporting that I have gained 1,000 fans would be impressive if I did it in a day, but it would be much less impressive if I achieved this over the course of a year (depending on your business). Setting terms in advance helps maintain agreement in the evaluation, and it provides sets of data to compare.

For instance, measuring Q1 (the first three months) against Q2, Q3, and Q4 provides natural breaks in the data for most businesses. Measuring a second year provides additional data sets over time, and so on. Consistent time periods and frequency provide easier comparison and improve the perception and acceptance of the data. I see some clients measure every day, and I see others measure once a month. No matter how you agree to measure, just do so in advance. Interpreting the numbers or the level of success after the fact leaves you vulnerable to interpretation.

How to Identify Goals

For some, goal setting is easy, or the goals are already defined for them. For those who need help in setting goals, I have two options, depending on your culture and style: the analytic or the esoteric.

Being SMART About Your Goals

In 1981, George T. Doran wrote an article in *Management Review* addressing "the importance of objectives and the difficulty of setting them.*" He introduced "a S.M.A.R.T. way to write management's goals and objectives" that has become a mainstay in management and marketing.

SMART Goals

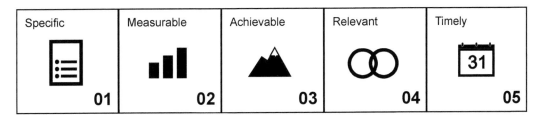

SMART is a mnemonic to remember that goals must be:

1. *Specific* – Target a specific area for improvement
2. *Measurable* – Quantify an indicator of progress
3. *Achievable* – Explain how you will achieve your goals
4. *Relevent* – State what realistic results can be achieved
5. *Timely* – Specify when the results can be achieved

Specific: SMART goals should be simplistically written and should clearly define what you are going to do and when you are going to do it. This means you must point out with clarity and detail exactly what it is that you would like to achieve (the more detail, the better). Using my company goals, my SMART goals would be:

1. Specific – My company will invest to create a social media platform on Facebook, LinkedIn and Twitter.

2. Measurable – We will share one message a day for three months to build an audience of 1,000 people for each social media network. The audience will consist of 50% Decision Makers, 25% Influencers and 25% Referrals.

3. Achievable – I am responsible for the direction of the content, my assistant is responsible for developing it, posting according to a communications plan and engaging with the community. We will both review the performance of each site twice a month and make corrections to the communications plan.

4. Relevant – We have set a goal of five new retainer clients generating $500,000.

5. Timely – We will repeat this process for 12 months and measure and report on the revenue generated from new conversations within social media.

This example is a simple demonstration, and that's intentional. I have read pages and pages of blah-blah-blah that was difficult to understand and that was open for interpretation. By all means, say what needs to be said and address what needs to be addressed. You can go into detail and depth, as necessary, but I've found less is more.

Side Note: There's a saying I tell my writers, "The more words you use, the less important each one is." It's always a challenge to get people who are paid to write to do less of it, but I find it to be effective. My designers are taught to take away as many elements as they can while still communicating what they need to get the message across. Both get them to the same place.

Specific

A specific goal has a much greater chance of being accomplished than a general goal. Vague or generalized goals don't provide sufficient direction. Stating, "We want to be successful using social media" isn't a very clear goal. However, stating, "We want to sell 100 products in three months" is crystal clear.

Specifics have a quantity and a time limit. Get where you want to go by defining precisely where you want to end up.

To set a specific SMART goal, you must answer the six "W" questions:
1. **Who:** Who is involved?
2. **What:** What do I want to accomplish?
3. **Where:** Identify a location.
4. **When:** Establish a time frame.
5. **Which:** Identify the requirements and constraints.
6. **Why:** Provide specific reasons for accomplishing the goal.

My company would answer the question as follows:
1. **Who:** Myself and my assistant
2. **What:** Generate five new clients and $500,000 in new revenue
3. **Where:** Facebook, LinkedIn and Twitter
4. **When:** 12 months
5. **Which:** Clients must be generated from social media activity or from past clients
6. **Why:** To meet revenue goals for the year

Remember, your goals are determining the "what." The "how" is a strategy you will develop later.

Measureable

Goals should be measurable so you have tangible evidence you accomplished the goal. Invest the time to develop a process you will use to measure your progress toward the attainment of your objectives. Usually the entire goal statement is a measure for the project, but there are typically several short-term or smaller measurements built into the goal. Establish concrete criteria for measuring the progress toward the attainment of each goal. Include the number of fans, followers, amounts, dates, and the like in your goals so you can measure your degree of success. When you measure your progress, you stay on track, you reach your target dates, and you do what is required to reach your goal.

To determine if your goal is measurable, ask yourself:
1. How much?
2. How many?
3. How will I know when I accomplish my goal?

Your answers should be quantifiable. If you can't answer this question, you can't measure the progress toward accomplishing the goal.

Achievable

You must believe you can achieve your goals. You can attain most any goal when you plan your steps and establish a time frame that allows you to execute those steps. Goals that may have seemed far away and out of reach eventually move closer and become attainable, not because your goals shrink, but because you grow and expand to match them. At the same time, make sure it's possible to achieve the goals you set. If you set a goal you have no hope of achieving, you will only demoralize yourself and erode your confidence. By setting realistic yet challenging goals, you hit the balance you need. These are the types of goals that require you to "raise the bar," and they bring the greatest personal satisfaction.

You must be able to answer the question: "How will this goal be achieved?"

Relevant

To be relevant, a goal will represent what needs to be accomplished. Relevant goals set direction, motivate the team, and move the organization forward. A goal that supports or that is in alignment with other goals would be considered a relevant goal. Setting inconsistent and unconnected goals only wastes your time and resources. Goals should measure outcomes, not activities.

A relevant goal can answer "yes" to these questions:
1. Does this seem worthwhile?
2. Is this the right time?
3. Does this match our other efforts/needs?
4. Are you the right person?
5. Is it applicable in the current socioeconomic-technical environment?

Some have argued the "R" in S.M.A.R.T. should be "Realistic." This means that logically—given your time, money, resources and level of skill—you will be able to achieve these goals successfully. If any of these is lacking, then you either need to improve your time, financial situation, skills, and resources or simply set a different set of goals.

Timely

A goal should fall within a time frame. With no time frame tied to it, there's no sense of urgency. Your goal is probably realistic if you truly believe you can accomplish it. Additional ways to know if your goal is realistic are to determine if you have accomplished anything similar in the past or to ask yourself what conditions would have to exist to accomplish this goal.

A time-based goal will usually answer the questions:
1. When?
2. What can I do today?
3. What can I do six weeks from now?
4. What can I do six months from now?

Collaborative Goal Setting

Collaborative goal setting is a group exercise to get every contributor on the same page. The group consists of all the stakeholders (the people who have some interest in developing your social media strategy) and the work is developed as a group with contributors being active participants. This is the essence of "collaboration."

This approach includes a series of questions publicly (synchronously) discussed that addresses where the business has been and that will help determine where the business is going. If you can't have a synchronous discussion, then document and share the answers (asynchronously) amongst your team. Track changes on the document to note the differences in word selection, opinions, assessment, information, data, etc. Honestly, you don't get the same dynamic without the group participation, but sometimes you have to do the best you can. Use the multiple perspectives you'll likely receive to further discussions in order to come to some agreement. Until you do, you cannot move forward. If you do, be forewarned: you will do so on an unstable foundation.

Sample Questions

History: What is the history of the company? When did it begin, what was it doing and who was involved? What made the product or services unique? Who were the customers, and why did they buy from this company? What has the company accomplished that it is most proud of? What is it known for? When people think of the company, what comes to mind? Continue with questions that follow this path and document the responses.

Today: How has the company changed? Has it changed at all? What do you do differently today than you did when you began? Who are the stakeholders—the people who have the most to gain from the success of the company? Who are the customers today—and are they different than in the past? What is different about the marketplace and the companies competing inside it? Continue with questions that follow this path and document the responses.

Vision: Where do you see an opportunity for your company? What do you want to do with your products and services in the future? How will your customer base change? How will you respond to deal with a changing customer? How will your company change, and what can you do to position your company for success?

Issues: What are the issues your company is facing today? What are the issues in its future? What can you do about it today? What can you do about it in the future? What will you require to address these issues? Will you be able to get what you require? Why or why not? What happens if you do not acquire these resources to address your issues?

Goals: Given the history of your company, where you are today and where do you want to be in the future? What can you do to achieve the results you have identified as important for your success? Write down each action item, and order them so you'll know which have to happen first in order to accomplish all your goals.

Metrics: For each action item, determine how you will measure its progress over time to demonstrate your success (think positive). Discuss these with a colleague and consider what they have to say. Revise them based on their feedback and your further thinking. When you're done, do the same with your team to gain a common understanding of your goals and how you will achieve success.

EXERCISE : Identify Your Goals

As an educator, I know applying what you have learned to something relevant to you right after you've learned it helps students better comprehend the material. As a consultant, I know my clients are much more excited to get to the part where we talk about how what I share impacts their business. We'll do both.

This exercise will apply what you have learned today to your business in an effort to help you identify your goals. Don't wait for somebody else to start this exercise, and don't worry about not getting it right. Focus on understanding this step of the process, and learn how to apply these exercises, as needed, to succeed.

1. Choose SMART Goal Setting or Collaborative Goal Setting

Choose one of the goal-setting methods to identify your goals. Draft a first pass at SMART Goals, or take a pass at the Collaborative Model (yes, by yourself—for now). Follow the process described in this chapter until it is completed. Do not take shortcuts, do not improvise, and do not, by any means, create a hybrid of the two (you're not making up a process, you're using one). If the first method doesn't work out, try the other.

2. Document Your Goals

Type out everything you think and organize the information in an outline that follows the model you've chosen. If you're reading this on a plane with no battery power left, you can write it out. However, you end up moving so much of the information around that it is much more efficient in a Word document.

From everything you've written, organized, and understood, identify and prioritize your goals. Depending on how many goals you've identified and what's required to achieve them, you may consider addressing goals in separate phases: a different time, a different budget, perhaps a different market. The point is, you don't have to address your goals all at once. You should only address those you know you can achieve.

3. Confirm the metrics used to measure the progress toward your goals.

Each goal will have a different opportunity for measurement. Address each goal and confirm what you will use to measure the progress based on the metrics you have available. Consider the activity necessary to achieve your goals as you set benchmarks.

Congratulations, you now have real goals and a way to know how you're doing.

Resources

To download S.M.A.R.T. Goal and Collaborative Model templates, (Word document) visit the book website at http://SatelliteMarketing.com.

References:

Doran, G. (1981). There's a S.M.A.R.T Way to write management's goals and objectives. *Management Review,* 35-36.

Sinek, S. (2011). *Start with why: How great leaders inspire everyone to take action.* New York: Portfolio / Penguin.

EDWARD R. MURROW

"The newest computer can merely compound, at speed, the oldest problem in the relations between human beings, and in the end the communicator will be confronted with the old problem, of what to say and how to say it."

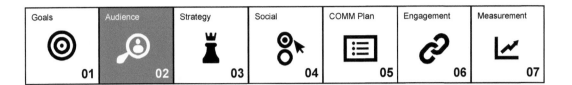

STEP 2

Understanding The Audience

Understanding your audience has always been the single most critical component of any successful strategy, and a social media strategy is no different. Knowing with whom you're speaking determines what to say and how to say it.

Most businesses can't say "everybody is our customer" (not even the cable company) as there are basic criteria that reduce "everyone" to categories with segmented characteristics.

Your audience is people. Whether you call them prospects, suspects, customers, or advocates, they are all people with whom you are trying to communicate to reach your business goals. They are men, women—maybe even kids—of different ages, incomes, ethnic backgrounds ,and geographic locations. They (and others) may be current users of social media and could potentially become part of the network you will create.

To fully understand your audience, start by detailing the different people within your audience. Think about the different prospects, the different customers, the different suppliers and resources that want to engage: trade associations, colleagues, partnerships, the media. Even regulatory bodies like the government and industry-specific organizations may have a part in your social media success. Budget permitting, hire a research firm to gather the empirical data. Accounting for all of your potential audiences is critical, and knowing as much as you can about them is the key to successful communication.

> *Some of you will skim this and think it's too hard or too much work. Remember what I said earlier—if you're not going to do the work, then you shouldn't be here. - kp*

Audience Profiles: Demographics (Quantitative)
Demographics is simply the quantifiable, numerical data you can collect about your target audiences. Most of the demographics I look for include:

- Title
- Age
- Gender
- Education
- Experience
- Knowledgebase
- Environment
- Geographic Location

Title: Knowing the title of the people you're trying to reach makes it easier to profile and easier to identify where those people may be. There's an obvious difference between a C.E.O. and a M.O.M. CEOs will be on LinkedIn and Twitter, while mothers will be on Facebook and Pinterest. There are not-so-obvious differences between a CEO, a CFO (Chief Financial Officer), and a CMO (Chief Marketing Officer). All of them might have profiles on LinkedIn yet participate in very different parts of the social media network. A CEO may participate in a LinkedIn group by sharing posts and leadership messages from his or her company. A CFO may have a profile but not be as active, and a CMO may participate in marketing groups and share content from the company. Three very different pieces of information could be estimated just by knowing the title.

Age: At one time, age was a valid indicator of your audience potential on social media. Today, this is not so much the case because of the adoption of social media into our culture and most other cultures throughout the world. Currently, 97% of all U.S. Internet users between ages 18–29 are active on social media. Although the percentage decreases by age group (93% of ages 30–49, 88% of ages 50–64, 57% of 65+), everyone is represented.

Age now tends to indicate social media preferences. Like television, specific channels are seen to provide general audiences both B2B and B2C businesses are looking to attract. If my clients are trying to reach children 11–13, then we start looking at Tumblr and Instagram; we're not looking at Facebook. Although Facebook is the largest social media networking site in the U.S., it doesn't deliver children 11–13 as well as Instagram or 14–17 year olds as well as Twitter (PEW Research 2013). Why? Because their parents are on Facebook, and the last place kids want to hang out being kids is a place where their parents will also be.

That being said, be careful. It's easy to let demographic assumptions lead you into making false determinations about your customers, social networks and their online behavior. Check current statistics to get the updated information on audience share by social network, and check more than one source for corroboration. The more specific information you have about your target market, the easier it will be to identify the appropriate social media sites, create an authentic and appealing online presence, and determine the best overall communication strategy for your marketplace.

Gender: Male or female, you can get to both using social media – they're just not always in the same place. *TIME* magazine had declared (Wagstaff 2012), "Men are from Google+, Women are from Pinterest"—a parody of the book *Men Are from Mars, Women Are from Venus* and a commentary on the inherent differences between genders on social media. At the time, 72% of users on Pinterest were women, so the generalizations today are based on learned statistics. As with any valid research, use current numbers when selecting your social media. Trends, by definition, shift like the sands of the desert. What may be there one day may not exist tomorrow.

Education: The differences in education have always impacted the type of messages I'd develop. A target audience of high school students has a differ language and points of reference than an audience of college students. MBAs even differ from those, and so on. Using the "wrong" words and poorly selected examples could make your message miss its mark or defeat the purpose of an important branding statement.

Environment: Where does your audience use social media: At home, At school, At work or On the go? Understanding their environment helps you understand how social media is used in their everyday life as well as how to best develop your messages to be successful. An audience at work may have access to more types of media, while the mobile users may access more video and pictures on smaller screens. Just think about where they are when they meet you; just as they will, there is a time and a place for each type of content.

Geographic Location: If you're a services company, are you interested in customers outside your service area? If you're a brick-and-mortar consumer company, are you interested in targeting prospects outside the reach of your physical locations? If you're an online store which doesn't ship outside the U.S., are you interested in Canada? The Internet connects millions of people, but not all of them are part of your audience. Knowing where they are in relation to your business helps limit the scope and the work needed to communicate.

Additional demographics could provide race, income level, an average purchase, home ownership—almost any numerical data. Cumulatively, this information will help you better understand your audience and provide the answers you need to make informed decisions about your social media strategy.

User Profiles: Psychographics (Qualitative)
Psychographic information considers the variable, qualitative, amorphous aspects of your target market.

1. What do they know about us?
2. What makes them tick?
3. What's in it for me? (WIIFM)

Psychographics address personality, values, attitudes, interests, and lifestyles. Sometimes referred to as IAO variables (interests, attitudes and opinions), psychographics can be contrasted with demographics, behavioral variables (such as usage rate or loyalty), and biz-graphic variables (such as industry, seniority and functional area). This information includes what companies your prospects work for, what position they hold within the company, how long they've been there, and how influential they are within the organization. Additionally, any information you can gather pertaining to purchasing behavior, major influences, or even computer usage patterns can be very helpful in refining the vision you have of your target market.

Knowledgebase: What does each of your audiences already know about you? What do they know about your competition? What do they know about your industry? These current levels of knowledge are helpful in categorizing the different types of users you'll work to address. If you're in sports, there's the general public that knows about your team, and there's a portion that has been to a game. Some tailgate, some have season tickets, and the knowledge they each have differentiates them in a conversation. Knowing how many of who are in the room directly impacts how many statistics and hall-of-fame factoids you throw out, right? The same goes for any business.

Experience: What has your audience's experience been with your product or service? Good, bad, indifferent? What about other products like yours? Many clients are brand loyal or bring stereotypes to services, like divorce lawyers, the cable company, or medical marijuana users. No offense, but did you react to at least one of these? If so, you know what I mean. Be honest about your customers—they don't all love you—and categorize their experience (new, repeats, lifetime, etc.) to develop an accurate audience profile.

Psychographics also address how your customers see themselves. Many researchers believe that because psychographics originate from a customer's self-identification, they're more relevant to a marketer than demographic information. We see obvious examples of self-identification in the social media that users select, and in the profiles they create to represent themselves. The username, often not their own but that of aspiration or admiration, differentiates online personas. The image selected to represent the user is not always a current photo but a picture from glory days past, with a significant other or a cartoon or hero from yesteryear. These compilations shape the individual and their personal brand to give the user a sense of placement in the social community.

The lack thereof does the same.

> *One of the interesting things about social networking is that while most people are fairly close-mouthed about their demographic information, they're not at all shy about psychographic material. They provide a lot of information if you just look for it. - kp*

User Profiles: Role Play

In theory, you should have a very good idea of the people you are trying to reach and the social media you're going to use to reach them. Now it's time to test the theory.

You have enough information where you can now role play (yes, role play) as each type of user profile. Pretend you are your audiences—each of them—and emulate how you think they act on social media. Consider what they do on each social media channel and what you would have to do to get their attention. For some of you, this will be funnier than others—and that's okay, because there is usually some truth in humor (that's what makes it funny).

If you're struggling with the concept of role playing (and need a good laugh) watch Mel Gibson in *What Women Want.* Didn't see the movie? Watch the trailer online. I want you to get into the role of each of your audiences to understand what it is like to be them (but you don't have to put on the pantyhose—watch the trailer).

When you're done laughing, think about your customers—again—and work to answer these questions.

1. *Where are your audiences already on social media?*
2. *What is their primary social media, secondary? Where do they never go?*
3. *What are they doing there? How often do they participate?*
4. *How do they view your company?*
5. *How do they use your products and services?*
6. *Where do you fit into their lives?*
7. *When they see your company on social media, do they care? Why or why not?*
8. *When they visit your social media profile, what do they do first?*
9. *What do they do second? Why?*
10. *Why would they want to engage with you? In what areas do you align?*
11. *Why would they NOT want to engage with you? Where are the disconnects?*
12. *How do you get them to like, follow, subscribe? To engage? To refer? To buy?*

For me, the role-play of a Decision Maker looks like this:

Target Audience: Decision Makers

- Decision Makers have profiles on LinkedIn. They may have a Twitter account or a Google+ profile, but they are not active participants on most social media. They have a profile because business says they have to have a profile to look contemporary and represent their role within their company. They connected to their existing network when they created their profile and accept connections from new people they meet offline but are open to new connections from online engagement.

- Decision Makers will use LinkedIn as part of the vetting process when I approach their company to provide services. The link to my profile will be included by a Referral in an email introducing me or in an email from an Influencer I have met and discussed the potential of working for their company. They will review my profile for professional experience and education, and they will read the Summary section for a synopsis since most people scan, they don't read. Decision Makers will look for people we both know to make inquiries before we meet. If they know someone, they will send him or her a LinkedIn message or an email asking for background. If I don't pass this review, they are hesitant to schedule a meeting.

You should be able to genuinely profile your audiences and defend your answers to others while they challenge your assumptions. I strongly encourage a good dialog among your team about each of your audiences. Even with clients who go into this telling me they know their customers, they've had the same customers for years, or we just did some research, etc., we have all learned something new from this exercise.

EXERCISE

Understanding Your Audience

Building from what you've learned in identifying your goals, start to document your current understanding of the audience by creating a list of each type of user profile. Segment each audience by general characteristics, but if important subtleties exist, label them as such.

- Target Audience A _____

- Target Audience B _____

• Target Audience C _____

For each target audience create a profile including what you know about:

• Target demographic:	• Education:	• Knowledgebase:
• Title(s):	• Environment:	• Psychographic:
• Ages:	• Geographic location:	
• Gender:	• Experience:	

Based on the profile you created, role play as each user on each social media channel. The more empathetic you can be, the more successful your social relationship may become. Document your observations and the key points in your social experiences.

• Role Play: A _____

• Role Play: B _____

• Role Play: C _____

> *When I complete this exercise, I share my documents with someone outside of my team for feedback. I listen, and I take notes. Many of my colleagues work in similar fields, so they know something about the people I'm profiling. They help me identify areas I missed or confirm the assumptions I have made. - kp*

When available, I share the profiles with samples of the groups of the people I'm profiling. Different than a focus group, I'm sharing with people what I see. It's a conversation starter between myself and my target audience—and I take a lot of notes. It's much faster than a focus group, and I find you get more authentic insight.

After you make any necessary edits to your user profiles, this step is completed. You'll cycle back through these at some point with some new data of your own, but for now, you can proceed confidently since you understand your audience.

Resources

To download User Profile templates (Word document) visit the book website.

References:

Wagstaff, K. (2012, February 15). Men Are from Google+ , Women Are from Pinterest | TIME.com. Retrieved November 7, 2014, from: http://techland. time.com/2012/02/15/men-are-from-google-women-are-from-pinterest/

"A plan, even the greatest of plans, is not a guarantee for results."

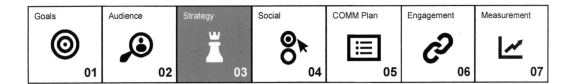

STEP THREE

Creating Strategy

At this point in the process, you know what you want to accomplish (refer to established Goals), and we know the people in your audience (refer to User Profiles). So how do we get these people to help accomplish your goals?

This is where the strategy comes in.

Darwin Had a Theory

Strategy is generally defined as a high-level plan to achieve goals. What are not generally defined, however, are the conditions of uncertainty that exist in achieving goals.

A good strategy will include a well thought out step-by-step of how a business is going to accomplish its goals. It will use the resources available within the budget agreed upon based on what it has learned from past experiences and what it knows today from best practices—but there are still no guarantees. A plan, every plan, even the best plan, is a best guess of what will happen in the future. It is not a purchase agreement for results.

There may be the likelihood in the plans you'll develop or a probability or some degree of predictability, but know that nothing in business is certain. Be prepared to tend to your plan, to monitor the success of your strategy by evaluating the metrics assigned to each goal. As you learn more, you'll adjust the plan in response to the new information and experience. A good strategy is well represented as a "living document," a document that will change, for the better, over time. Remember Darwin's Theory of Evolution: Over time there is a "natural selection" that facilitates evolution. It's not the strongest or the most intelligent who will survive, but those who can best manage change.

The Formulation of Strategy by Process

Like most businesses, my company has an allocated amount of time and resources to achieve its goals. To develop my strategy, I will apply what I already know to formulate an action-oriented plan. This plan will act as a strategy that answers the question, "How will I stay on task, on time, and on budget to achieve my goals?"

For my company, I have three goals:

1. Create social media profiles for my business that perpetuate my existing branding.
2. Build my social network from the users of select social media sites.
3. Use the social network to generate leads that turn into clients.

My Target Audiences include:

- Decision Makers with Budget
- Influencers
- Referrals

To address each of my goals, I create a Strategy Overview—a 100,000-foot view of the actions I think I can take to achieve each objective. I write down each of the big steps and a little description of what each means or includes. If I have options, I document those options and discuss them further as each develops. Documenting this thinking captures the information I need to visualize what I'm planning and serves as a mechanism to share with my team for feedback.

(Prioritized Goals) + (Ordered Actions) = Engagement

Here's an example of how I worked through creating my strategy and a model for you to create yours. (Just think - Prioritized Goals + Ordered Actions = Strategy)

Goal 1: Create social media profiles for my business that perpetuate my existing branding.

Review Audience Profiles: Understand the people and their relationship with our company and services.

Select Social Media: Based on audience profiles developed for Facebook, LinkedIn, Twitter, Google+ and YouTube.

Develop Social Media Profiles: Brand profile according to corporate identity standards using provided fields and functionality. Personalize / brand / secure username to reflect company branding (based on availability). Include all current relevant data and links in each social media profile. Install content, as needed, to populate containers and present an established profile.

Integrate Communications: Include social media icons and addresses throughout communications platform (website, email, advertising, marketing, etc.).

If I do all of these things in this order, I will have completed my first goal. The completion of the first goal prepares me to address the second—I can't start bringing attention to our company until we're prepared to make an acceptable impression.

Goal 2: Build my social network from the users of select social media sites.

Content Marketing: Develop a stream of content that positions our company as subject matter experts. Share the content across the social media platform (all sites).

Content Integration: Repurpose content developed for social media, and cite the source of the content to drive traffic, fans, followers, subscribers.

Audience Integration: Invite audiences from other channels to participate with us on social media. Email addresses, mailing lists, customer lists, and contacts from other social media profiles inform the people we already know that we have a new social media profile.

Outbound Networking: Use our personal profiles to connect with users who match our target criteria (decision makers, influencers, referrals), then introduce our company and services page on the platform to grow the company audience (followers, fans, subscribers). Offer assistance as a subject matter expert for their questions as incentive to connect.

Achieving this goal will require ongoing work, but once the first cycle is completed, we'll be prepared to start working toward the next goal.

Goal 3: Use the social network to generate leads that turn into clients.

Share content from company social media with our network of connections. Describe briefly, share a fact, and let them know what we think. Once a week, ask an open question about an article to start a public conversation.

Join groups where we can demonstrate our subject matter expertise in front of Decision Makers and Influencers. Add comments to group questions (as appropriate). Share company content with commentary (as appropriate).

Identify Decision Makers that match target criteria (CEO, CMP, VP, B2B, $10–50 million annual sales). Contact connections to identify a process for introducing our company.

Schedule presentation, track results.

Measuring Our Success

Each month, we review our activity and the leads-to-sales statistics. Quarterly, we measure the results against the term (12 months) established to learn where and how we can improve the strategy. Over time, with consistent execution and proper measurement, we develop a successful strategic approach to achieving our goals.

That's how I developed my strategy for achieving our business goals. Of course, there's a lot more to figure out, but at this point we're really just trying to identify reasonable options for a strategy to achieve each of the goals. Think of the formula like this:

$$\frac{(\text{Prioritized Goals + Ordered Actions})}{(\text{Time + Measurement})} = \text{Strategy}$$

Of course, there are numerous ways to develop a strategy, depending on what your business needs and what you're prepared to invest.

SWOT Analysis

SWOT stands for strengths, weaknesses, opportunities, and threats. The SWOT Analysis was developed in the 1960s by a research team at Stanford University including Marion Dosher, Dr. Otis Benepe, Albert Humphrey, Robert Stewart, and Birger Lie (thanks, fellas).

Funded by Fortune 500 companies to learn why corporate planning failed, SWOT was developed to serve as a strategic planning methodology to gather information about internal and external factors in achieving an objective or goal. With this analysis, a business can better:

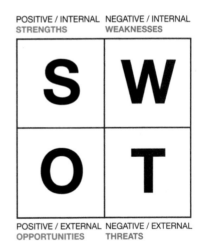

POSITIVE / INTERNAL NEGATIVE / INTERNAL
STRENGTHS   WEAKNESSES

S	W
O	T

POSITIVE / EXTERNAL NEGATIVE / EXTERNAL
OPPORTUNITIES   THREATS

• Examine goals and objectives before investing time and money
• Define competitive advantages and opportunities for growth
• Identify prospects, profitability, and product development
• Prepare for the competitors to respond, or even attack

In using SWOT Analysis, there's a tendency to view like items with the same weight and impact on the objective (Google "POWER SWOT" for more details). Consider how these items could impact the weight of your contributions:

Personal Experience: How does the CEO contribute to the SWOT analysis? He brings leadership, experiences, skills, knowledge, attitudes, and their beliefs to the audit. Their perception of an issue will impact the SWOT dramatically more than a Sales Manager.

Order: It's called SWOT for a reason—because the process addresses strengths, weaknesses, opportunities, and threats in that order. Some suggest that working out of sequence adds improper emphasis and misleads the group against the objective (you decide).

Weighting: Not all contributions are created equal, and weighting them equally (one is as good as another) is unfair and illogical. Assigning grades or percentages to each contribution to differentiate between the good and the not so good is appropriate.

Emphasize the Details: Details, rationales, and justifications are not always included in a SWOT worksheet (or they are just verbally shared in passing). Documenting all of the information, written and verbal, contributes to making informed decisions.

Rank: With your contributions weighted and details included, a SWOT analysis provides context and value. Selecting a strategy leveraging the greater assets and ideas provides a sense of confidence in investing and moving forward.

> *It's kind of confusing that they refer to this four-square diagram as a "SWOT Analysis." What it really does is serve as an instructional model: think about this, then think about this, then think about this, etc. It facilitates the examination of different facets of achieving the objective for a sampling of different perspectives to discuss (i.e., great conversation starters). The "Analysis" part of a "SWOT Analysis" comes in these discussion and conclusions of this information. - kp*

Executing a SWOT Analysis

Strengths are internal attributes of the product, service, or company that help in achieving the objective. Consider:

- What do you do well?
- What do you do better than most?
- What do you do better than anyone?

Strengths include both tangible and intangible attributes and are within the control of the company.

Weaknesses are internal attributes of the product, service, or company that are not helpful in achieving the objective. Discuss:

- What do we do poorly?
- What should be improved?
- What should we avoid given what we know today?

Weaknesses are factors within the control of the company and are areas where there can be an improvement.

Internal factors (things that are usually within your control) focus on your past performance, your present strategy, your resources, and your capabilities. This is where you have the control to make a difference in your situation. Consider these as the buttons and levers that can make dramatic changes in your business: add a service, develop a product, or expand into another market. You can view internal factors as either strengths or weaknesses,* but it depends on the objective (you really have to keep this in mind—*it depends). What may be an advantage for one objective may be a weakness for another. As hard as it may be, it is imperative to maintain objectivity when answering questions about your organizational strengths and weaknesses.

Opportunities are external attributes of the product, service, or company that are helpful in achieving the objective or in meeting the goal. It is the "stuff" that propels the company from where they are to where they want to go (i.e., growth).

- Where can you find or create a real competitive advantage?
- What are the big trends in your business?
- What changes can you make that lets you provide something the competition can't?

It's also helpful to assign all of these opportunities to a timeline, as some may make themselves available before others.

Threats are external attributes of the product, service, or company that are not helpful in achieving the objective.

- What obstacles do you face?
- What could your competitors do to take your customers or your market share?
- What technology is a threat to your current capability?

External factors (things that are more than likely out of your control) can be viewed as either opportunities or threats depending on the objective or the goal (just like it matters to internal factors). An opportunity for one objective may be a threat for another, and, like internal factors, objectivity is critical. An attitude of "everyone stinks but us" is the fastest way to make this entire exercise a waste of time.

Starbucks: A Grande Decaf SWOT Analysis

Most everyone knows the coffee company Starbucks, and most have had a cup of something from one of their many locations. Since so many are familiar with this simple business, it makes for a good example of how to apply the SWOT analysis to a business and how to better understand how you will apply it to yours.

Mission Statement: Starbucks posts, "Our mission: to inspire and nurture the human spirit —one person, one cup and one neighborhood at a time."

Background: Starbucks Coffee Company is the leading retailer, roaster and brand of specialty coffee in the world. From Starbucks' 1971 founding in Seattle as a local coffee bean roaster and retailer, the company has expanded rapidly. In the 1990s, Starbucks was opening a new store every workday, a pace that continued into the 2000s. The first store outside the United States or Canada opened in the mid-'90s, and overseas stores now constitute almost one third of Starbucks' stores. In 2013, Starbucks reported 19,000 stores worldwide and 14.9 billion U.S. dollars in total revenues.

Objective: How can Starbucks keep coffee customers from choosing McDonalds?

Strengths: What are Starbucks' strengths in combating McDonalds?
- Branding: Starbucks is a global asset.
- Capital: Well funded; money to do what they want.
- Product Development: Ability to develop products in music, food, personal, equipment, and cause-related marketing. Satisfies buyer's need for self-esteem.

- Cross-Promotions: Everyone wants to partner with Starbucks.
- Training Program: Quick to implement new services.
- Customer Service Program: Consistently rated "outstanding."
- Employee morale is high, proud, badge of honor to work in some communities.
- Distribution: Coverage of target market is huge.
- Pricing: Able to purchase in great quantities to achieve low pricing (costs).
- Wireless Internet: Attracts day workers, students, loyalty, and an enduring ("busy") look and feel.

Weaknesses: What are Starbucks' weaknesses in combating McDonalds?
- Highly competitive industry: always someone coming for them (big dog syndrome).
- Premium product in a tough economy: How to continually justify?
- Slow to respond: too big, too expensive.
- Pre-conception of price points ("Starbucks is expensive").

Opportunities: What are the opportunities Starbucks has to compete?
- Smaller Portions / Sizes: Same great product but smaller serving reduces price point.
- Expanded Food: Offer more compatible foods to upsell customers while they are already there; breakfast, lunch, brunch, dinner, snacks, take-home.
- Promoting Locations: "You are only five minutes from this location."
- Feature-Rich Locations: mini-mart, store, super store, mall.

Threats: What are the threats to Starbucks from McDonalds?
- McDonalds has more locations, bigger reach, deeper pockets.
- McDonalds' brand is value-based.
- The economy is a variable—what happens when things get "good" or "worse"?
- Culture changes based on factors like the economy.

As much as the SWOT matrix itself captures the information, it is in the collective discussions and analysis of individual efforts (like the Starbucks sample) against the objective and goal that generates the real value. The people you include in your discussion should represent a cross-section of people from different backgrounds you trust. You'll be discussing some very sensitive material, so you'll have to be comfortable talking about product / service specifics, admitting the weaknesses and potential threats your company currently has—as-is—in the marketplace.

How Business Creates Strategy

Most big businesses are familiar with the development of a formal strategic plan. It includes all of the information its management needs to know to make an informed decision about moving forward and everything it needs to know about the return on its investment.

- Executive Summary
- Elevator Pitch
- Company Mission Statement
- SWOT Analysis*
- Goals*
- Key Performance Indicators* (KPIs)
- Target Customers*

- Industry Analysis
- Competitive Analysis & Advantage
- Marketing Plan
- Team
- Operations Plan
- Financial Projections
  *Previously addressed in detail

An executive summary provides an overview of the complete proposal that readers can quickly understand. Depending on its application, the executive summary can be used to assess an opportunity without investing a great deal of time—a go/no-go step for the audience to determine if they need to learn any more.

An elevator pitch serves a similar purpose, although it is usually developed for external audiences. It's a quick introduction to simply present a business idea and its value proposition (also known by Marketing as "WIIFM"—What's in it for me?). The term "elevator pitch" comes from sales lore—a good salesman should be able to deliver his business opportunity in the time he had a prospect trapped in an elevator. If the pitch were successful, the conversation would continue as they both walked out the elevator on the same floor. If it were not, the doors would close on the deal.

The company mission statement is just that—a statement. It is a succinct presentation of the company's goals, philosophies, or tenets that communicates what the business stands for to employees, customers, and their community. It is not an advertisement or a marketing brochure, but it is part public relations. A business's actions will be measured against its mission statement, so it's essential to choose words wisely.

The goals of a business strategy are well defined, just as we've explored earlier. Sell your product, introduce your service, or steal customers from a competitor. Without a goal or objective in mind ahead of time, a business will run the risk of this being a very futile exercise (i.e., a complete waste of time).

Gathering information to support the research of a market size, the price per ticket, or the consumer spend on a product in a category annually prepares a business to complete an accurate analysis of the real opportunity and to set realistic goals. Where you gather this information can make a difference in how much and what type of information you end up analyzing. Consider using a mix of different resources to shape a fair and accurate picture:

- C-Level executives (try to be objective, okay?)
- One-on-one interviews (don't lead them, ask open-ended questions)
- Customer Focus Groups (no incentives, please)
- Input sessions with Sales (Hey, who knows your customers better? Nobody.)
- Industry Analysts, Media and Associations (people who see the big picture with little or no prejudice)

Prepare specific questions in advance that relate to your product, service, or company as you identify goals. Open-ended questions will produce a conversation that you'll have to sift through to find what you're looking for but may also include some issues and items that you had overlooked. Try to avoid any gray areas that someone could misinterpret or that could come off as argumentative. Be specific (as the situation demands), and your goals will be on target.

Key Performance Indicators (KPIs) are the indicators used to gauge the success of the strategy. Some call them metrics, others measurement, but all will tell you how well you're doing and how much farther you need to go before you reach your goals. Sharing this in advance of reporting provides an opportunity to confirm the measurement tool as well as the criteria to be considered successful.

What we call "audience," business calls "target customers," and it implies that there's a purchase to make. Depending on the goals, this may be more accurate, but they both mean the people you're trying to reach. The demographics and psychographics will demonstrate the understanding the business has of its customers and will be critical in building the foundation for this strategy.

An industry analysis demonstrates the same breadth of understanding, but for the marketplace in which the business operates, including key companies, trends, challenges, and opportunities. This big-picture view of the total market opportunity (all customers in an industry) usually includes reports on revenue and statistics for each segment of the business (i.e., product type A, B, C, etc.) over time and any projections for the future.

The competitive analysis and advantages will be the result of the SWOT Analysis, providing insight into strengths, weaknesses, opportunities, and threats of current and potential competitors. Often overlooked or based on assumptions, this analysis is critical for the development of an effective strategy and efficient implementation. Ongoing monitoring will provide an ongoing stream of intelligence as your business moves and your competitors respond.

This is a great place for a rubric. All too often I see businesses make assumptions about their competitors in their marketplace, or overlook / underestimate their real competition. Unless you have very fresh data that is applicable to your business goals, I'll suggest you to do the work. - kp

The marketing plan is a plan within the business plan. Both are essential in helping the business organize their operations and provide milestones and metrics to determine their success. The difference is that a business plan looks at every aspect of the business, while the marketing plan details the specific actions the business must complete to reach its marketing goals. A marketing plan can include:

• **Executive Summary:** A succinct overview of the complete proposal used to assess the market opportunity.

• **Target Markets:** An overview of the total market opportunity and the segments within the industry you will be targeting. Like our audience profiles, they'll reference demographics and psychographics.

• **Unique Selling Proposition:** The message presented by a seller as the reason that one product or service is different from and better than the competition. In an overpopulated marketplace of parody products, it's very difficult to stand out in the crowd. Unless you can identify the "unique" in your sales messages, you cannot expect that your customers will either. Role play as your customer to learn what motivates their behavior and buying decisions, and uncover the real reason customers buy your products over a competitor's.

• **Pricing & Position Strategy:** The pricing of your product in the marketplace must align with the position marketing has created for it. If it doesn't, it may cause questions in the minds of prospects that prohibit their purchase.

• **Distribution Plan:** A detail of how products and services will be distributed to customers. In-store, online, direct mail—how many channels are available and which would your customers select?

• **Offers & Promotions:** Special programs created to draw attention to the products and services to attract new customers or reward current customers to purchase again. Free trials, money-back guarantees, bundled services, and limited time discounts help move prospects into suspects and suspects into customers. Promotions can be considered for the channels they're delivered upon, like online, in-store, and partner programs or a process within the business, like referrals, conversions, and customer retention (just to name a few).

•**Marketing Materials:** The marketing collateral—website, brochures, direct mail, business cards, point-of-sale, etc.—used to promote the products and services. Including samples of the proposed materials can help create or clarify a vision for the people trying to evaluate the plan. When well executed, experienced professionals will attest to their effectiveness in swaying opinion toward program approval.

• **Financial Projections:** A detail of the financial investments and expenses, as well as the projected returns. Yes, there is an expected return, i.e., this shouldn't cost you anything. If this does become a cost, you'll have to address why this makes sense. Although projections are a best guess at the beginning of a plan, they can help identify which investments can generate the greatest return in the shortest amount of time contributing to strategy decisions. These financial projections can help translate established goals into specific targets, providing an ongoing feedback-and-control tool to detect and identify challenges before they happen.

A team is the people who work for the business and are responsible for the actions that contribute toward the work to complete the goals that achieve the results. Identifying the players on the team presents an understanding of the work, and an appreciation of the skill set and experiences can provide an evaluation and appreciation for the plan's potential success.

The operations plan links the strategic plan with the activities of the organization. This plan includes an overview of the milestones to complete the plan, the metrics for success, and the term of the business activity it represents. An operational plan includes goals, actions, budgets, responsibilities (organizational chart), KPIs, and reporting—enough of the right information to determine, where we are now, where we want to be, how we get there, and how we measure our progress.

Financial projections address the two most important factors: how much will it cost and what can we expect to make? Financial information should be provided to represent the projected revenue, balance sheets, cash flow, and capital expenditures for a multiple-year term (three to five years). For the first year, expect to include monthly / quarterly reports that demonstrate how the operations are implemented on budget and the revenue is realized on time.

Failing to Plan Is Planning to Fail

There's a number of appropriate business sayings when it comes to planning, but my favorite remains, "Failing to plan is planning to fail." As appropriate, in my opinion, is, "Paralysis by analysis." Identifying the balance between everything you could include and what you think you need will be somewhere in the middle.

EXERCISE: Draft a Strategy for Your Business

In this exercise, you'll draft a strategy for your business that builds off the goals and audience profiles already completed. By using the SWOT Analysis, you'll identify the strengths, weaknesses, opportunities, and threats for your business. This information will provide the basis for your discussion, evaluation, and prioritization. Selecting a portion of these to address within a specified time parameter will provide a framework for your Executive Overview—a 100,000-foot view of the actions needed to achieve your business goals.

Complete a SWOT Analysis for Your Business

Within the SWOT Analysis, you'll analyze the industry, the competition, and the advantages for each business. There are literally hundreds of questions that are specific to your company, and the products and services that you sell to your customers in each vertical market. Think about these big-picture items as you prepare to discuss your business.

- Products and Services: What are we selling?
- Process: How are we selling it?
- Customer: To whom are we selling it?
- Distribution: How does it reach them?
- Finance: What are the prices, costs, and investments?
- Administration: How do we manage this?

In most SWOT Analyses, the competition is considered when answering these questions. Analyze each of them (as they relate to your company) to provide detail on the market as a whole. Remember, these questions are just conversation starters—jump in with your thoughts after you get some momentum.

- What capabilities does your company have?
- What could you improve?
- What does your company do better than anyone else?
- What resources do you have access to?
- What do your customers see as your strength?
- What do your customers see as your weakness?
- What should you avoid?
- What do you need to create a sale?
- What do you do to lose a sale?
- Where are your gaps in capabilities?
- What is your unique selling proposition (USP)?
- What are your resources and your assets?
- What is your experience in the market?
- What is your location and / or geographic reach?
- What is the quality of your product, your price, and your value?
- What are your accreditations, certifications, or qualifications?
- What are your processes and / or procedures?
- What technology do you use?
- What staff, training, and management does your company have?
- What information do you have or can gain access to?

Consider these questions for your discussion of the Opportunities and Threats. Document the answers within your SWOT Worksheet (or in a document of your own).

- What are the good opportunities you have today?
- What are the trends in your market?
- What are the recent changes in your technology?
- What changes have been made in your government regulations?
- What has changed with your customers recently?
- What events are available in your marketplace?
- What new developments are in your marketplace?
- What has happened to your competition recently?
- What new trends are becoming apparent?
- What are the global influences in your industry?
- Are there any new markets or niche markets available?
- What are the new products in the marketplace?
- Is there any new information or research in your industry?
- What could you do with your partners, your agencies, or your distribution channels?

- What volume of production could you produce?
- Are there opportunities within the seasonal change or from the weather?
- What is your competition doing differently than you?
- How do the government or legislative issues affect your business?
- What would the loss of key people mean to your business?
- What strategic alliances would impact the lead in the marketplace?

Pairing SWOT Factors to Formulate Strategies

Another idea generation technique is to pair different categories together. Ask your group to discuss:

- SO Strategies (Strengths + Opportunities Strategy)
- ST Strategies (Strengths + Threats Strategy)
- WO Strategies (Weaknesses + Opportunities Strategy)
- WT Strategies (Weaknesses + Threats Strategy)

For example, your Strength is "your team has strong employee morale" and your Opportunity is "competition is losing stamina." A resulting strategy could be to put on more pressure (to get the competition while the gettin' is good).

Now do the same for SW Strategies, WO strategies, and WT strategies. Remember, these are exercises (mind games, mental exercises, etc.) to stimulate ideas and discussion of relevant topics. We do them in order to test an objective or a goal (so don't take it so seriously, okay? Just roll with it and you may be surprised what you get.).

At the end of the discussion, decision makers can review the results to determine whether the goal or objective is attainable. If it is, take the next steps toward achieving your goal. If it is not, then create a new objective or goal and repeat the process (it does go faster the more you start thinking like this). It may seem like a tedious process, and it is. But it is also a thorough process that helps your business make critical decisions for its, and your, future.

Keep in mind, there are no right or wrong answers—only answers. This entire exercise is designed to get you to look fairly at your entire business situation.

Draft an Executive Overview

Based on the results of your SWOT Analysis, draft an Executive Overview of the actions you will have to take to reach your audience and achieve your goals.

(Prioritized Goals + Ordered Actions) / (Time + Measurement) = Strategy

Goal 1
  • Action / Time / Measurement

Address each of the items, with brevity, expected to be addressed in a business strategy, including:

  • Company Mission Statement
  • SWOT Analysis (highlights of results, Industry Analysis, Competitive Analysis and Advantage)
  • Goals*
  • Key Performance Indicators* (KPIs)
  • Target Customers*
  • Marketing Plan*
  • USP
  • Pricing & Positioning
  • Distribution
  • Offers & Promotions
  • Marketing Materials
  • Team
  • Operations Plan
  • Financial Projections

Repeat for each additional goal identified by your team.

References:

Division of Administration, State of Louisiana. *Operational Plan: Format, Guidelines, and Instructions FY 2000-2001.* (2000). Retrieved from:
  http://doa.louisiana.gov/opb/faf/OPFormatWord_FY01MWLayout.pdf
Multiple Sources. Retrieved from: http://www.statista.com/topics/1246/starbucks/
Starbucks Mission Statement retrieved from:
  http://www.starbucks.com/about-us/company-information/mission-statement

Not all social media is created equal, and in your audience's mind, they may not all serve the same purpose.

STEP 4

Selecting Social Media

Based on your goals and your audience, you're now looking to select the social media networks and sites that can support your strategy.

As you begin, a special consideration should be given to your audience's perception of social media. Not all social media is created equal, and in your audience's mind, they may not all serve the same purpose. Consider that just because you're looking for them does not mean they're looking for you or expecting uninvited guests.

If you were sitting in the coffee shop, and a man begins making his way around to all the tables, handing out a flyer and a free CD to each group, chances are you're not going to care all that much when he makes his way to you. You're sipping coffee, the guy's offering free music, you're a nice guy, the flyer's talking about a show that maybe you and your friends will want to catch later. It's all good. His interaction is both relevant and appropriate, and you are, at the very least, gracious.

Take that same guy, with the exact same stack of flyers and CDs, and bring him into your favorite fancy restaurant where you're wining and dining an important client. How are you going to feel when he starts making his rounds and approaching your table? You're going to become uncomfortable, even annoyed—in your mind, it's not the time or place for such activity. The same type of consideration should go into selecting the time and place you'll start building an audience for your business.

Each type of social media provides unique opportunities to support your strategy by helping reach your audience and by supporting the actions you've identified as important.

Social Networking sites enable people to connect with other people—to establish a channel of communication. These sites are helpful in building relationships with current customers and creating engagement with new prospects by sharing messages, information, and links to other resources on the Internet. They are the basis of a social network and can be the core of a business's social media platform.

Content Sharing sites help people share different types of information and media. Pictures, graphics, video, presentations, audio, music, et al.—all types of content for all types of people looking for a type of media or subject matter.

Collaboration sites help people create influence, generate capital gain, or collaborate on an enterprise level. Working one-on-one or in groups, working side-by-side or in shifts, people can contribute to a common effort to achieve a business's goals.

Start with What You Know

Like other media, we can begin selecting social media by demographics and psychographics, identifying the general locations of the different types of people in our audience.

To support my goals, we're looking to build a network of CEOs and VPs, 35–55, of national companies. We could start on LinkedIn and Twitter, just like we would start with CNN and MSNBC with television or ESPN and PBS with radio (depending on the size of the company). I know we can get to this audience there because my general industry media "buzz" is reporting stories and statistics on that job title and age (demographics) on those social media networks.

With a little research, we find data that supports our assumptions, like *Forbes* magazine's report, "CEOs are most active on LinkedIn (1)." In a survey from PEW* of CEOs at America's 500 highest-grossing companies, 27.9% (or 140 CEOs) have LinkedIn accounts (1). The same report shows Twitter has far fewer CEO users, with just 5.6% (or 28 CEOs) of the top 500 companies. Surprisingly, the number of CEOs on Facebook is slightly higher than Twitter, at 7.6% (or 35 CEOs).

Nowhere does this data show we should look to Instagram, Pinterest, or Google+, so investing in those social media networks would not bring us closer to our target audience.

With basic research, we've identified LinkedIn, Facebook, and Twitter and can statistically prioritize each (based on the data supplied). With more research, we'll find even more relevant and timely data. It would help us make an informed decision about the types of preferred content for our audience (i.e., pictures are the most engaging content on Facebook (2013)) and the potential reach for collaboration using different functionality from each type of social media (i.e., only 47% of CEOs participate on social media (2013)) to initiate a relationship. Like any research, consider the year the data was published, and, the source.

You can find current statistics for social media user demographics by using Google and a decent set of keywords like "Social Media Demographics by Job Title" or "LinkedIn User Profile Demographics," depending on what you're looking for. Social media networking sites may provide information on their user demographics as part of their advertising options. - kp

Like my business, most businesses will use more than one type of social media to reach its audience. Why? Because some people watch TV and other people read the newspaper— people have preferences for media consumption, and it's hard to get to everyone using one channel. Businesses are often tempted to just say, "Let's use them all" (figuratively speaking, since it would be impossible to be on every social media site): Don't.

Every social media profile created is an opportunity and also a responsibility. It can even become a liability if unattended. Assuming too many commitments on social media has the ability to engulf your budget and detract from your focus. Prioritizing your social media will help you think through a strategy now and the resources it will require in the future.

Developing a Platform, One Profile at a Time

The premise for participation on any social media network is the creation of a profile to represent the user to the other users in the network. A collection of profiles across multiple networks creates a social media platform—multiple points of contact and varying types of communications between you and your multi-segment audience.

The user profile can represent a person or an organization in the form of a profile, page, channel, or a group. Anybody can create a profile. When you fill out the sign-up form, most social media services provide a step-by-step guide that facilitates the creation of a basic personal profile. It may even find the people you already know and provide some tips to get you started contributing to their community.

Review The Terms of Service—Every social media site has a different Terms of Service agreement, a published policy for users that states what you can do and what you cannot do. It may speak to your rights, assignment of rights, and what happens to your content when you upload it to their site. A Terms of Service agreement is legally binding and may be subject to change with no prior notice. The agreement will dictate how the service stores the user's personal data, payment information, or contacts. It will also dictate your activity and messages, as a business, within the community. Know, in advance, what you're getting yourself—and your business— into before you get started. - kp

Developing a social media profile for a business to achieve specific goals is more complex than just filling out the blanks of a profile (set up wizard or no set up wizard).

To start, the functionality of a social networking site (usually) requires a unique username to identify one user from another, an image to add a "face" with the name, and some basic information about the user to present them to another user. Look to logos, taglines, photos of your team, pictures of your products, and location to provide the basics. As users build their network with other users, a list of connections is (usually) created as a reminder to you of whom you know, a shortcut to find them, and a representation to others of whom you are in the scheme of things. Messages between users, both public and private, are the text and links to other resources to attract attention and to facilitate communication. Its opportunity is dependent upon the functionality provided by the social media service (you can't "like" something if there isn't a "like" button) and the communications assets you have to build it (you can't add a cover photo you don't have in an electronic format).

Content sharing sites, by definition, require content to share. Functionally, content must be added to a profile before it can be shared with other users. Profiles can be configured to represent the business with strategically placed (and re-purposed) content from existing brochures, advertisements, websites, public relations documents, branding, design, multimedia, and events as new "social" media. Pictures, graphics, video, presentations, audio, music, et al. are (usually) displayed in real time to connections or scheduled for a later release and can be organized for future reference by the public (in albums, lists, or galleries).

Purposeful interaction between users is the basis for collaboration sites. Depending on the strategy, different types of collaboration can be applied to complete the actions required to reach your goals. The interaction builds the network, the users create a group and the result of the interaction contributes towards social capital between users for future collaboration.

It continually surprises me that still some people and organizations put little thought or systematic planning into developing social media profiles. Seriously, it's not that hard, and if you're not going to put a little effort into this, then you probably won't put much effort into the rest of this. - kp

Building a Personnel Profile

A personnel profile—a profile that presents a person as a representative of a business—should include the information a customer (or would-be customer) would want to know about you before deciding to contact you or engage with you online. Transparency in identifying a person as a representative of the company is critical so other people understand you're speaking from that role. Consider your audience: What are the most important things they would want to know about you as a person representing your business? In their mind, there is a list of compulsories—a foundation from which to build. Start with those your industry would require.

If you're in a B2B market, for example, a prospect might want to know your role within the organization. Someone who is seeking out your organization to order 150,000 new widgets might not want to spend time in a relationship with the HR manager (they want someone in Sales). On the other hand, someone who wants to work for you or to supply your seasonal business with temporary labor might be very interested in forging a strong relationship with your HR manager. It depends on who they are and what they need.

Understanding the Difference between Personal and Personnel

Just as your audience may not be prepared to engage your business on a social media network, your employees may have their own hesitations. This is a discussion for you and each employee to address any expectation as part of their employment, an explanation of how this coincides with their job requirements and with the rights and privacy of them as a person.

This is, for some people, a new discussion. There was a time when there was a strict separation for people between their private life and their professional life. Back in the day, you knew George Wilson ran the Hometown Insurance Company, he was married and had some kids, but that was likely all you knew about George. He was a family picture and a name on a calendar that came in the mail each year, and that was about it.

Those days are largely gone. In an era of relationship marketing, where customers make business decisions based upon who they know and trust, social networking has put the model on steroids. It's ramped up to the nth degree, and any test better read "positive." There is a blurring of the lines between personal and personnel as customers have increasing expectations of authenticity and connectivity from the people with whom they do business.

Customers don't just want to know that George runs the Insurance Company. Customers (and prospects) like knowing about George's personal interests, like his passion for raising Border Collies. They're interested when one of those collies has puppies. They want to see pictures with his kids and they may even be interested in how George thinks having puppies is like growing a family in a blog post (an analogy to remind his audience about his business and their insurance needs) even though what George does in the course of his daily professional life has absolutely nothing to do with dogs.

There should also be a conscious decision regarding how much personnel interaction people are expected to engage in during the course of social media networking for business if they choose to participate. In my opinion, the correct answer here is *not* "all the time" but I'll suggest that it isn't "None at all," either. As a business owner, I appreciate the people who work for me towing the company line, in some part, to support the company that helps them succeed. Successful social networking, content sharing, and collaboration for a business hinges on genuine engagement with your audience with the people who represent the businesses as points of contact. Successful companies, like mine, have learned an audience wants to know they're talking to genuine people with real lives and personal interests, not just corporate bots set up to tweet three times a day.

You have to show up for something good to happen. Make each personnel profile look and feel accessible; it is counter-intuitive to social networks. Accessibility is very valuable and some people just want to connect: provide them that opportunity. You just might be pleasantly surprised by who reaches out and the reason why. - kp

Representing The C-Suite

Being a member of the C-Suite or another influential person within your organization can present a unique set of opportunities to represent the business, initiate relationships, and create engagement.

A C-level personnel profile should represent the credentials of the position, justifying the title and demonstrating why the business has them in that position. A profile with a big title (Chief Executive Officer) is expected, in many circles, to have a history of previous positions that may have led to his or her current role. Starting out with CEO as the first and only position will often raise a question of credibility (how did they get this job?) or minimization (they must be self-employed). Based on the options available, providing descriptions of the responsibilities, time served in the role, and achievements earned helps clarify the position and demonstrates good judgment on behalf of the organization.

The profile should reflect some personal interests and values as well to demonstrate authenticity and individuality. It's not just another company marketing tool, it's a human representative of your company.

The perception of the person in the personnel profile will help initiate relationships through invitation and acceptance. A credible profile demonstrates the position and its authority; activity of the profile demonstrates the leader is a contemporary and active channel of communication: both are signs of life to someone looking to connect.

An active profile will help create engagement based on the type of activity. More activity, like communicating publicly, sharing content, and collaborating within group discussions will generate more exposure to other people, in turn creating more engagement with new people. The demonstration of the leadership role of the company, related content, and subject matter expertise supports the perception of the profile by the audience. Over time, this perception grows the influence with the audience and the social capital of the leader. Cumulatively, the C-Suite can become a valuable asset for the company and a key contributor to the success of the business goals.

> *Make it easy for the C-Suite to contribute. In most cases, this will not be their core competency or responsibility, depending on age and industry. If you make it easy for them (or their designate) to participate, they will. - kp*

Creating Perception

Many people look at the creation of a social media profile at its face value (wow, it's a social media profile), but what we're really building is perception.

The profile is the first impression of your social media life. Whether you run into your audience or your audience runs into you, they're going to walk away with an impression. Just like in the real world, the success of that perception depends on you.

They may not know you yet. Like the first day at a new high school, there isn't anyone who knows anything about you except what you tell them. If you know who you want to be, all you have to do is be that person and—ta-dah—that's how they see you. As long as you can maintain and manage the perception, the perception will be real (i.e., "Perception is reality."—Lee Atwater (1)). Just make sure that nothing shows up after the fact that dispels your myth, like the mean girl that went to your old school or a picture of you before your makeover. Being exposed for being less than authentic almost always carries social ramifications—just like high school—none of which end up being good.

When developing personnel profiles, consider issues like:

- What do our customers want to know?
- What do our customers need to know?
- How will customers use this information?
- How could this information be interpreted by our audience?
- Do we want our customers to know this about our personnel?

Your audience may know you already, so they'll bring past knowledge, impressions, and experiences with them. Three things can possibly happen when you reunite online. One: They will think less of you—you just don't look as good as they remember. Two: They will maintain the same impression—you look and act the same as offline. Or three: They will think more of you—you really look good on social media. Your choices and efforts will determine which.

Social Media Policy & Guidelines

In an ideal world, every one of your employees would have a personnel profile to support your organization's goals: more hands, less work. The advantage of multiple points of representation, contact, and influence for your business could greatly impact the success of the program, depending on the strategy, but it may also create some unexpected challenges.

What happens when something doesn't go according to plan?

Every business needs, at a minimum, a simple policy defining the expectations of personnel representing the business online and within social media. This should exist as an understandable document that addresses the use of a personnel online presence and the expectation of the related activities therein. As the company size increases, so does the potential risk associated with employees and representatives discussing work and customers in a public forum.

A social media policy can set the expectations for behavior online as it relates to supporting a mission statement, company goals, or strategic initiatives. Identifying and discussing these issues in advance helps avoid the issues (they can't say they didn't know) and provides a metric to identify when the rules are broken.

• What happens if they misrepresent products or services?
• What happens if they get in an argument with a customer or competitor?
• What happens when the company receives a complaint?
• What happens when they share copyrighted or inappropriate content?
• What happens when they leave the company?

As an experienced HR manager would share, common sense is sometimes uncommon when it comes to employees and their activities in business. Published guidelines can help avoid legal issues by identifying them as such in advance, like divulging corporate secrets or linking the company name to activities, positions, or opinions, on which that the company has not provided guidance or approval. In a regulated industry, this could be disastrous. Sometimes things are intentional too. A good social media policy can also provide direction when legal recourse is necessary against employees for the actions.

As a social platform grows and profiles are created, so may pages where a community evolves. A public policy outlining the expectations for behavior for members can help prevent similar issues with non-employees. Setting boundaries early demonstrates that your community is managed, provides an example of the social etiquette expected, and can demonstrate the standards and ethics important to your business. The policy should offer points of contact for questions and issues and be dealt with in a timely manner.

One of the most overlooked policies is for administrators of the social media platform: rules and regulations for the people in charge of its success. Internally, Human Relations may have documentation for the performance of an employee, but externally they would not. As many companies outsource the development, execution, and management of their social media platforms, a policy defining the roles, responsibilities, expectations, use credentials, information stored on devices, content shared from client accounts—all potential issues—should be well defined before they need to be addressed in a crisis situation.

Profile Development Cheat Sheet

Before you jump in to start building your social media platform, take a timeout to think about some things. Gather the information you'll need to create a profile so when you do start, you can complete the task the first time.

Username: Select a username to represent your business: It's the name by which you'll be known by the social media network and how you'll be presented to other users. Will your customers know it's your business? Is it available on each of the social media networks you want to use now or in the future? Does it meet the character limit or restrictions for each social media profile? Are there any legal restrictions on its use?

Profile Image: Most profiles use an image to accompany the username, a square or rectangle GIF, JPG, or PNG (electronic graphic file formats) of a specific size or file size. How will you represent your business: logo, icon, product, mascot, or spokesperson? Think about how this image will display on all types of devices and if the options change from desktop to tablet to mobile.

What's the public name of the business, or what is the legal name required (with a ©, ™ or LLC)? What is the tagline or descriptive copy for your products and services? Is there a corporate address or multiple locations? Which, if any, should be included? Which contact information should be included and why? (If you present a channel of communication, expect communication on that channel.)

Text: From "About the Company" to general information about products and services, which of the existing copy from up-to-date websites, advertising, and marketing collateral is appropriate to include?

Links: If the opportunity exists to link to another site, which will it be? Should multiple links be available? Think about the origin of this social media profile and where it fits in the sales / marketing / support process—people from here should go where?

8-: What existing content is available? How much is available? Will more be available in the future? Pictures, articles, video, animation, commercials, music—which of these will support the goals for this program? Which will help create engagement with our target audience?

Connections (List): Is there a list of people with whom the business already has a relationship that can help identify connections on each social media profile? Customers, clients, prospects, partners, suppliers, association members—people the business already knows that would be interested in connecting on social media. Where is the list, in what format, and how can each social media profile use this list to help build the network?

Interaction: How will we introduce the business to the people on the list? What will be our first interaction? Why will they be interested in hearing from us? Will they be receptive to a social media connection? What could we do to create a positive first interaction?

Network: How will we manage the social media network? Who will be authorized to manage the social media profiles? Which devices are authorized to access the profiles, and are usernames and passwords allowed to be stored? What will they be, and what happens when we have to change them?

Group: Will we create groups for people to communicate, share, or collaborate? One group or multiple groups? Who will manage these groups? Who will be invited to participate in these groups?

Sales or Social Capital: What's the purpose of the social media? Are you (ultimately) trying to sell a product or service online, or are you just concerned with creating social capital? Whatever your goals, keep them in mind as you present each of the items available in the social media profile. Pennies make dollars, and each choice adds up to create your business's perception.

Exercise: Select Your Social Media

Based on your strategy, identify which types of social media would best reach your audience.

- Social Networking sites enable people to connect with other people.
- Content Sharing sites help people share types of information and media.
- Collaboration sites help people create influence, generate capital gain, or collaborate on an enterprise level.

Based on your current knowledge, detail which social media networks your target audience utilizes. Include why you think they utilize the network and how they utilize it for their own needs.

Based on research, confirm that your audience is available on the social media networks. Identify alternate social media networks for further research and discussion. Prioritize the social media and make your final selection.

Create a basic user profile for each social media network. Use the Profile Development Cheat Sheet to complete a first draft of each profile.

Congratulations, your business is on social media.

Resources:

Download the Profile Development Cheat Sheet from the book website.

References:

Adams, Susan. (2013). *Less Than a Third of Top CEOs Are on Social Media.* Retrieved from: http://www.forbes.com/sites/susanadams/2013/08/07/less-than-a-third-of-top-ceos-are-on-social-media/

Atwater, Lee. (n.d.). BrainyQuote.com. Retrieved December 12, 2014, from: http://www.brainyquote.com/quotes/quotes/l/leeatwater409179.html

Go-Gulf. (2013). *CEOs on Social Media [Infographic].* Retrieved from: http://www.go-gulf.com/blog/ceo-social-media/

SocialBakers.com. (2013). *Photos Make Up 93% of the Most Engaging Posts on Facebook.* Retrieved from: http://www.socialbakerscom/blog/1749-photos-make-up-93-of-the-most-engaging-posts-on-facebook

"The COMM Plan™ is a proven process model, based on best practices, to facilitate the development of an integrated marketing communications plan."

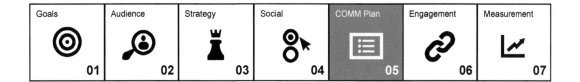

STEP 5

Communications Planning

Creating engagement with an audience over time doesn't just happen. Somebody executed a well-thought-out plan.

A successful communications professional will have a document that shows what they have planned, when it goes live, and how long it impacts their audience. Adding budgets and hours, you would have a document that keeps every department in the company on time and on task. With every budget dollar critical, it would be irresponsible not to have something in place.

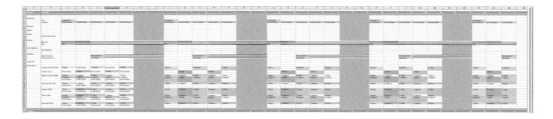

A communications plan is a detailed document that addresses how you will communicate with your target audience to achieve your goals: a 10,000-foot view of how a business integrates communications across all channels to its target audiences, providing a demonstration of strategy—in advance—for consideration, including hours, costs, and resources required. Shared throughout the company, everyone works from the same page to execute the tasks necessary to complete the actions that bring it closer to reaching its goals.

A communications plan demonstrates best practices from all types of communications: marketing, branding, advertising, social media, multimedia, Internet, public relations, events—everything. Each effort, internal or external, is examined for opportunity and integrated, when appropriate, with other channels to generate the greatest reach, the biggest impact, and the maximum return on investment.

Save Time, Save Money, Communicate Better

Day-by-day, a communications plan helps keep everyone on task, on schedule, and on budget. When used with an active project management system (like Google Docs) that supports desktop, laptop, tablet or mobile—everyone (internal and external) can have constant access to the plans, calendars, contacts, and files that they need to perform. Coupled with project management content and development, a well-designed communications plan steers the ship toward success.

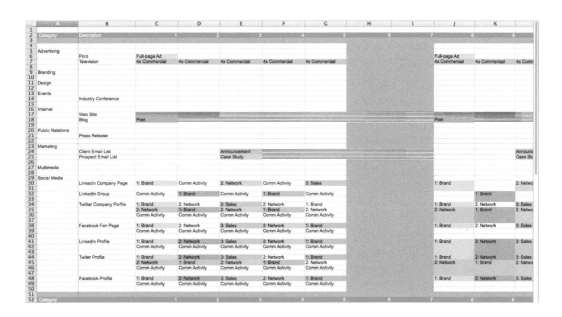

Month-by-month, a communications plan accounts for dozens of projects and directs hundreds of purposeful messages. Each project is scheduled and assigned tasks and responsibilities. Monitoring these tasks over time can identify meaningful information and realistic metrics so that at any given point, a confident answer can be given to the critical question, "How are we doing?"

Building a Model Based on Goals

In general, there are two types of communications I have with my audience: direct and indirect. The direct communication is what I first employed to create engagement: "Hi, my name is," and "Nice to connect, what are you working on?" I will also use direct communications when furthering the development of my personnel relationship, when I'm prospecting and when I'm developing my customer relationships (i.e., sales).

The indirect is the (marketing) communication oriented to my total audience: everyone to whom I am connected, and those to whom I am not but may be considering (and those considering connecting with me).

The indirect communication shared on my social network is purposeful—I don't post just to post—and it's planned in advance so I don't have to think about what to do every day on every day. Every planned message, shared link or media brings me closer to one of my established goals:

1. Create social media profiles for my business that perpetuate my existing branding.
2. Build my social network from the users of select social media sites.
3. Use the social network to generate leads that turn into clients.

In any given week, there are seven days I could communicate—someone is always online—but does it make sense to communicate every day? Like the philosopher suggests, "If a tree falls in the woods and nobody is there to hear it, does it make a noise?" If I post and nobody is online to see it, does it communicate? The answer from social media is (again) —it depends. It depends on your social media channel and it depends on your social media audience.

My audience is primarily C-level executives, and I know (from my research) that they are most active on LinkedIn. I need to stay in front of these people and I know they'll see (statistically) one out of every three indirect communications I share. If I share six, they will see two.

Days	S	M	T	W	T	F	S
LinkedIn	X	X	X	X	X	X	

I know (from my research) that my total audience (Decision Makers, Influencers, and Referrals) is available on Twitter every day and that it has a newsfeed faster than LinkedIn, so I'll need to communicate more frequently for my indirect communication to be viewed by my general audience. Twice as many posts to (statistically) insure the delivery of twice as many messages.

Days	S	M	T	W	T	F	S
LinkedIn	X	X	X	X	X	X	
Twitter	X	X	X	X	X	X	
	X	X	X	X	X	X	

With a better understanding of the communication requirements to reach my audience, I know how many messages I need to develop: 18 messages for two social media networks each week should bring me closer to my goals.

Mapping Actions to Goals

Using my goals (1, 2, and 3) as a starting point, I can determine what my messages will include by mapping my actions to goals thus ensuring my communication is purposeful.

Goal 1 = Perpetuate my brand.
Goal 2 = Build my social network.
Goal 3 = Generate leads that turn into clients.

I know I need 18 messages and that I have two social media channels, and for the most part a person in one network is not on the other (although over time this will change). What I share on one network can be shared (appropriately) on another to reduce the amount of content development required (nine messages) and to increase the reach of each message (more people will see each message). When one person is in both of my social networks, I will create multiple impressions (like when you hear an ad on the radio and then see the video version on television—one reinforces the other).

I start Sunday building my social network, Monday I generate leads that turn into clients, and Tuesday I perpetuate my brand. On Wednesday, Thursday, and Friday, I repeat the model because I like ending the week on my brand. If my prospects have an unsolved problem at the end of their week, I want them thinking about my company as a solution.

Days	S	M	T	W	T	F	S
LinkedIn	2	3	1	2	3	1	
Twitter	2	3	1	2	3	1	
	X	X	X	X	X	X	

I still have a requirement for a second message on Twitter so I can support the same goal or work toward a different goal. I choose different because I want to add some variety to keep my communications varied and interesting.

Days	S	M	T	W	T	F	S
LinkedIn	2	3	1	2	3	1	
Twitter	2	3	1	2	3	1	
	1	2	3	1	2	3	

The types of communication I share can also be based on my goals.

1. The types of communication that perpetuate my brand:
    a. Text: A statement about my company
    b. Text + Link: Information about the services we provide with a link to our website
    c. Text + Picture + Link: A statement about a picture of me and my clients with a link to work we developed together

2. The types of communication that build my social network:
   a. Text: Quotes and insights from me about what I see in communications
   b. Text + Link: Links to recent articles and research that support what I have said
   c. Text + Video + Link: A statement about an issue in my industry, a link to video contributing to this statement, and a link to connect with me (a subject matter expert) on the network to answer questions about the issue.

3. The types of communication that generate leads that turn into clients:
   a. Text + Image: Tips, insights, and information about our best practices
   b. Text + Link: A statement about a problem a client had, and a link to success stories about how we helped a client succeed
   c. Text: Opportunities to "join our conversation" and ask questions

With these nine different types of messages supporting my identified goals, I can update my communications plan to offer a variety of content throughout the week to keep my audience interested, and hopefully, engaged.

Days	S	M	T	W	T	F	S
LinkedIn	2a	3a	1b	2b	3c	1a	
Twitter	2a	3a	1b	2b	3c	1a	
	1a	2	3b	1c	2c	3a	

Think of your social media channel like a radio station. Do you want to hear the same songs over and over again, or do you like variety in what you hear? If you're watching a television channel and the same ads plays over and over, do you even see them at some point? By approaching the messages of a communications plan as "program development" you can create a much more interesting offering to your audience and increase the chance they will pay attention, over time. - kp

Much of this content I already have readily and steadily available; the rest I will have to identify or develop, but at least I have a basic model for communicating with my audience that scales (more channels, more messages) and gets me moving toward achieving my goals.

Academics have investigated the process of developing a communications plan from many perspectives, including, in one case, in achieving their own communications goals. A plan to help them plan their planning.

The Communications Unit within the Division of Diversity and Community Engagement (DDCE) at the University of Texas at Austin needed to keep its audience up to date on its own communications planning process. The goals of the department included:

1. Provide consistent and timely messages about the ongoing development of their strategic plan.
2. Engage staff in the process, especially by communicating opportunities for involvement in key decision points.
3. Ensure accurate, consistent, and frequent messages are delivered in a variety of ways that encompass different methods of communication.

The communications plan was initiated by providing a message (hard copy letter and email) to their audience announcing the effort and inviting members of their staff to become involved in the process. It also emphasized the importance of the project for their collective growth, ongoing work, and stability of the division (demonstrating WIIFM, or the "what's in it for me" to their audience).

The school provided a blog as a source for outlining their purpose, principles, and the monthly updates that would be made as the work progressed. Readers were notified via email every Monday that an update had been posted and encouraged to provide their feedback as comments on each blog post. Important dates related to the project were added to the department SharePoint calendar. Post cards were developed to reinforce the blog posts and electronic messages and to reach parts of their audience who prefer more traditional methods of communications. Face-to-face meetings were also scheduled into the communications plan to reinforce their commitment to "fellowship and connection," providing the ability to conduct an orientation, focus groups, and ongoing dialogue about the program and its progress toward reaching its goals.

According to the DDCE website, "The success of the strategic planning implementation relies upon the plan becoming an integral part of DDCE's work. Thus, it is important to regularly communicate with staff across the division on the work being done and accomplishments achieved through the plan. [We] have developed a communications plan to ensure strategic plan news and information is delivered to key audiences." Components of the plan included:

- Update Strategically Speaking blog and produce a public-facing blog.
- Include information in DDCE social media outlets, such as Facebook and Twitter.
- Provide information for new hires during the orientation process.
- Include updates in all-division staff meetings and senior staff/unit director meetings.
- Publish links to relevant information on DDCE websites.
- Publish an annual printed document listing priorities and accomplishments.

"The strategic planning process was intentionally designed to connect with the work of units and portfolios throughout the division and to encourage open communication among staff. Reflecting these goals, 84% of survey respondents indicated that the strategic planning process was effective (extremely, very, or somewhat effective) in recognizing and addressing the priorities of the work they carry out on a daily basis. Additionally, more than 90% of staff said that they felt comfortable discussing aspects of the process with members of the Planning Team."

Integrated Marketing Communications

In business, the use of coordinated messages over multiple channels is called "Integrated Marketing Communications." First defined by the American Association of Advertising Agencies in 1991, IMC was introduced as "a concept of marketing communications planning that recognizes the added value of a comprehensive plan that evaluates the strategic roles of a variety of communication disciplines—for example, general advertising, direct response, sales promotion and public relations—and combines these disciplines to provide clarity, consistency, and maximum communications impact." Later defined by the American Marketing Association, as "a planning process designed to assure that all brand contacts received by a customer or prospect for a product, service, or organization are relevant to that person and consistent over time" IMC has become the standard of business communications strategy.

IMC includes all types of marketing communications: Branding, marketing, advertising, design, public relations, multimedia, events, word of mouth, social media, the Internet: every type of communication and every derivative thereof. If it's a method or type of communication between one person and another, it can be included in the plan.

In *Advertising and Promotion: An Integrated Marketing Communications Perspective*, authors George Belch and Michael Belch write, "In our complex society, advertising has evolved into a vital communications system for both consumers and business. The ability of advertising and other promotional methods to deliver carefully prepared messages to target audiences has given a major role on marketing programs of most organizations. Companies ranging from large multinational corporations to small retailers increasingly rely on advertising and promotion to help them market products and services. In market-based economies, consumers have learned to rely on advertising and other forms of promotion for information they can use in making purchasing decisions."

"Before reading on, stop for a moment and think about how you would define marketing. Chances are that each reader of this book will come up with a somewhat different answer, since marketing is often viewed in terms of individual activities that constitute the overall marketing process. One popular conception of marketing is that it primarily involves sales. Other perspectives view marketing as consisting of advertising or retailing activities. For some of you, market research, pricing, or product planning may come to mind. While all of these activities are part of marketing, it encompasses more than just these individual elements. The American Marketing Association (AMA), which represents marketing professionals in the United States and Canada, defines marketing as, 'the process of planning and executing the conception, pricing, promotion and distribution of ideas, goods and services to create exchanges that satisfy individual and organizational objectives.' Effective marketing requires that managers recognize the interdependence of such activities... and how they can be combined to develop a marketing [communications] program."

Why Does IMC Work?

According to the Integrated Marketing Communications program at West Virginia University, "five major shifts in the worlds of advertising, marketing and media have caused an increased interest in (and need for) IMC. These include:

A Shift From...	Toward...
• Traditional Advertising	• Digital/Interactive Media
• Mass Media	• Media
• Low Agency Accountability	• High Agency Accountability
• Traditional Compensation	• Performance-Based Compensation
• Limited Internet Access	• Widespread Internet Availability

"These shifts are forcing organizations to look at the whole marketing picture, re-aligning their communications and seeing things the way the consumer sees them—as a constant flow of information from indistinguishable sources. Those who practice IMC are avoiding duplicate messages, capitalizing on the synergy among promotional tools, creating more effective marketing programs and maximizing ROI."

Most importantly, IMC makes sense because your audience is (usually) in more than one place. Look to the demographics of your audiences—the same info that told you your audience would be accessible on social media. What does your research show about reaching this audience via email? What about advertising using print, magazine, television, or radio?

The same Nielsen study that showed trust for social media (recommendations from people I know and consumer opinions posted online) also showed efficacy in other types of communications stating that they "completely / somewhat trust other types of advertising, including:

- Branded Websites (69%)
- Editorial Content in Newspapers (67%)
- Ads on Television (62%)
- Ads in Newspapers (61%
- Ads in Magazines (60%)
- Billboard / Outdoor Advertising (57%)
- Ads on Radio (57%)
- Subscribed Emails (56%)

"While TV remains the front-running format for the delivery of marketing messages based on ad spend, consumers globally are also looking to online media to get information about brands," said Randall Beard, global head, Advertiser Solutions at Nielsen. "On the flipside, earned advertising channels have empowered consumers to advocate for their favorite brands, something that shouldn't go unnoticed by brand advertisers."

No matter the scale, the strategy of integrated marketing communications should be included as best practices in every communications plan.

Developing a Communications Plan

Like most plans, there are logical steps in communications planning that you take to complete the process. Complete the steps, in order, and you'll complete the process, as designed.

Like most educators, I'm concerned about student learning outcomes from my teaching. Follow my exercises, as designed, and you will succeed. One part professor, one part Mr. Miyagi (i.e., *The Karate Kid*); some parts may sound like a textbook exercise and others may sound like "wax on, wax off," but each step in the process will impact the success of your business. I guarantee it.

A couple caveats from the podium: First, this only works if you follow the process. Improvising along the way voids my warranty that this will deliver a comprehensive, efficient, and strategic plan. Second, you only get out of it what you put into it. Take the responsibility for the work; then you can take the credit for its success. – kp

The COMM Plan™ is a proven process model, based on best practices, to facilitate the development of an integrated marketing communications plan.

Although there is great complexity in the execution of an integrated plan, there are four primary steps in the creation of a COMM Plan. The letters in the acronym depict the focus of each step: Channels, Opportunities, Messages, and Models.

1. **Channels:** Selecting the channels of communications utilized to communicate with the audience (i.e., Advertising, Marketing, Social Media)

2. **Opportunities:** Identifying the opportunities within each channel to reach the audience (i.e., print ad, customer survey, Twitter account)

3. **Messages:** Creating messages for each opportunity that maps actions to goals (i.e., advertise product to create interest, collect survey info for product development, share photos to build audience)

4. **Models:** Developing process models for each channel based on the messages and opportunities (i.e., applying information and insight to create an approach to communicating that can be repeated and tested over time)

Selecting Channels

Using the COMM Plan™ template (or a spreadsheet application), list the channels of communications selected to reach the audience.

- Advertising
- Branding
- Design
- Events
- Internet
- Marketing
- Multimedia
- Public Relations
- Sales
- Social Media

Numbers (1–31) across the top of the columns provide a month-at-a-glance view. Highlight the columns for the weekends throughout the month to quickly identify the weekdays, and denote any other days for special consideration, like holidays or special occasions.

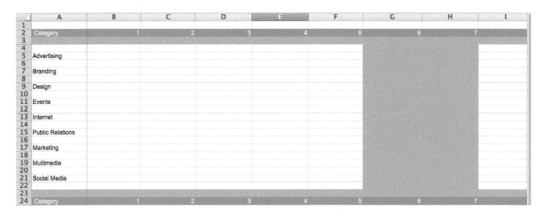

View the entire spreadsheet to see an empty matrix of monthly communications opportunities, providing a big-picture perspective of the potential communications available to reach the audience.

Zoom into the spreadsheet to easily view a week at a glance (days 1–7), and scroll to the right to review each other week of the month. Use a column titled "description" (between the categories and the first day) to add specific social media under its category title, keeping like items together. Add the social media profiles for the business, then add the personnel profiles for any contributors. This will provide a list of every social media page or profile available, which enables you to evaluate how each can do their part, and how all can work together.

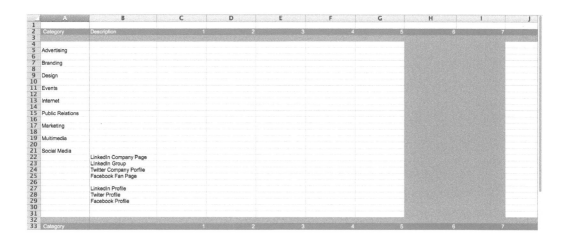

Next to the other categories, add a description of the other channels already being used to communicate—print, TV, events, website, blog, press releases, email—everything. We need to identify every communications tool available.

Identifying Opportunities

Opportunities: Identifying the opportunities within each channel to reach the audience.

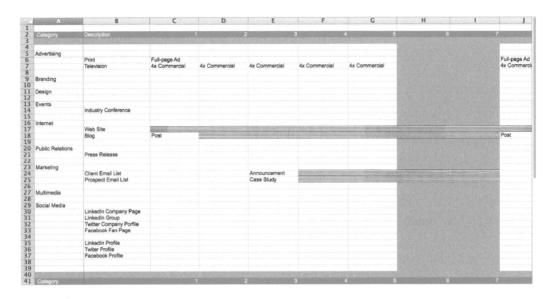

If the asset is available every day to your audience, like a website or a blog, mark the row from the 1st to the 31st as active. As your Google Analytics will (probably) report, somebody visits your website every day, so it actually does communicate every day. It's also something that can be updated, as needed, to support and coordinate with other assets.

If an asset is only available on a specific day, like a print ad in a daily newspaper, then denote the day the ad is available. If the asset will be available for more than one day, like a week of television commercials, then mark each accordingly.

If an asset is distributed on a specific day, denote the day of the release and estimate how long the asset will remain an asset. The impact of communications to an audience tends to include more than just the day it was released. For instance, a blog post may be published on a Monday but referenced as long as the blog is available. An email, on the other hand, may be sent on a Wednesday but be expected to remain an asset for only a week—after so much time, it gets deleted.

When each of the channels has been recorded and all of the assets have been represented, you'll have a 10,000-foot view of how you currently communicate with your audience, the frequency of communications, and a better understanding of the messages you're currently using. You'll also have a better understanding of the assets and opportunities available to integrate with your social communications.

Messages

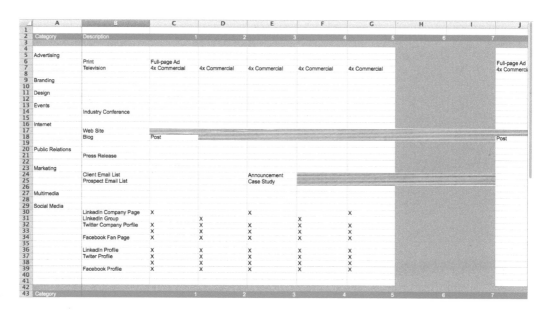

Viewing the first week of the model, focus on the list of the social media profiles available, identifying which days of the week your business will communicate with your audience and how often. Higher frequency channels—those that require messages more often—are added to each social media profile as an additional row to differentiate one message from another. Messages may be designated by day part (a.m. or p.m.), consider time zones (EST, PST), and even specific times of the day (9 a.m., 4 p.m.). Defining these variables now provides specificity for execution and the differentiation for comparison during testing and measurement.

As you predict the need for each profile, pay attention to the cumulative requirements of the week. Since each decision impacts the requirements for the weekly process model, the costs to communicate and the hours to manage for the month will replicate as well.

Mapping messages and content to goals makes your communication purposeful: you're doing something for a reason. This strategic approach to communications means there's an expected result of investing in a message—when we say "hello," we expect people to say "hello" in return. We're expecting engagement. Over time, each message will bring you closer to creating relationships that turn into conversations, making forward progress toward completing the tasks required to reach your goals.

	A	B	C	D	E	F	G	H	I	J
2	Category	Description	1	2	3	4	5	6	7
5	Advertising									
6		Print	Full-page Ad							Full-page Ad
7		Television	4x Commercial	4x Commercial	4x Commercial	4x Commercial	4x Commercial			4x Commercial
9	Branding									
11	Design									
13	Events									
14		Industry Conference								
16	Internet									
17		Web Site								
18		Blog	Post							Post
20	Public Relations									
21		Press Release								
23	Marketing									
24		Client Email List			Announcement					
25		Prospect Email List			Case Study					
27	Multimedia									
29	Social Media									
30		LinkedIn Company Page	1: Brand		2: Network		3: Sales			
31		LinkedIn Group		1: Brand		1: Brand				
32		Twitter Company Porfile	1: Brand	2: Network	3: Sales	2: Network	1: Brand			
33			2: Network	1: Brand	2: Network	1: Brand	2: Network			
34		Facebook Fan Page	1: Brand	2: Network	3: Sales	2: Network	1: Brand			
36		LinkedIn Profile	1: Brand	2: Network	3: Sales	2: Network	1: Brand			
37		Twiter Profile	1: Brand	2: Network	3: Sales	2: Network	1: Brand			
38			2: Network	1: Brand	2: Network	1: Brand	2: Network			
39		Facebook Profile	1: Brand	2: Network	3: Sales	2: Network	1: Brand			
43	Category		1	2	3	4	5	6	7

Number your goals: 1, 2, 3, etc. You can also include short codes for an easier reference, like Brand, Network, or Sales. Review the opportunities matrix (all the blank cells) and allocate each of the goals to one of the messages. The more messages a goal needs to be reached, the greater number of messages dedicated to that goal. Prioritization of goals, compared to one another or based on time to complete, helps provide a rationale for one over another and the number of messages dedicated to each. No matter how you represent them on your plan, the real need is to stay focused on the goals and to distribute their focus throughout the week.

	Category	Description	1	2	3	4	5	6	7
5	Advertising								
6		Print	Full-page Ad						Full-page Ad
7		Television	4x Commercial	4x Commercial	4x Commercial	4x Commercial	4x Commercial		4x Commercial
8									
9	Branding								
11	Design								
13	Events								
14		Industry Conference							
16	Internet								
17		Web Site							
18		Blog	Post						Post
20	Public Relations								
21		Press Release							
23	Marketing								
24		Client Email List			Announcement				
25		Prospect Email List			Case Study				
27	Multimedia								
29	Social Media								
30		LinkedIn Company Page	1: Brand		2: Network		3: Sales		
31		LinkedIn Group		1: Brand		1: Brand			
32		Twitter Company Profile	1: Brand	2: Network	3: Sales	2: Network	1: Brand		
33			2: Network	1: Brand	2: Network	1: Brand	2: Network		
34		Facebook Fan Page	1: Brand	2: Network	3: Sales	2: Network	1: Brand		
36		LinkedIn Profile	1: Brand	2: Network	3: Sales	2: Network	1: Brand		
37		Twiter Profile	1: Brand	2: Network	3: Sales	2: Network	1: Brand		
38			2: Network	1: Brand	2: Network	1: Brand	2: Network		
39		Facebook Profile	1: Brand	2: Network	3: Sales	2: Network	1: Brand		

With a strategy of purposeful messaging in place, look for the opportunity to integrate social media with the other channels of communication. The message from a full-page ad in the newspaper can be repurposed as an update (JPG of the ad, copy from the headline) to a LinkedIn company page, a post with an image (same JPG of the ad) on Twitter, and a status update (text based on ad copy) with a (JPG) photo that gets added to an album on a Facebook fan page. In this example, you can increase the reach of the advertisement and amortize (justify) the cost of developing the advertisement since it is applied to more than one channel.

The personnel profiles can also be assigned to contribute to supporting the brand messaging by sharing the same image with a "personnel" statement, varying from the business but towing the company line, as a status update on LinkedIn, a post on Facebook, and a tweet on Twitter.

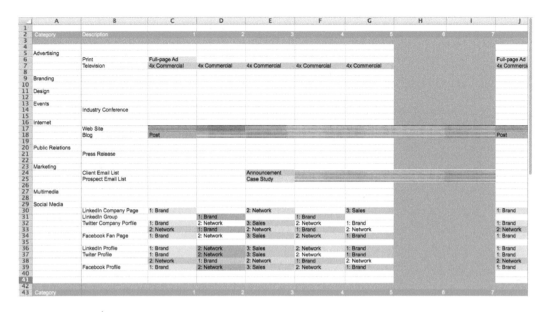

Continue to look for other opportunities to repurpose existing communications, like the example of television commercials:

- Add the television commercial to the company website to keep the content new for returning visitors.
- Share the television commercial throughout the week with the business audience on social media to support networking (audience building) and sales (lead generation) goals.
- Share the television commercial via personnel profiles to increase the reach of the business message, and use it as a conversation starter with the people in your business network.

Every type of communication—blog post, corporate announcement, or case study—can contribute toward the messages that help attract people to a social media profile. Every message is an opportunity to take action toward a goal and to build a social network. Every response—like, follow, or comment—can be an opportunity to better understand your audience and to learn how to engage with the different types of people within.

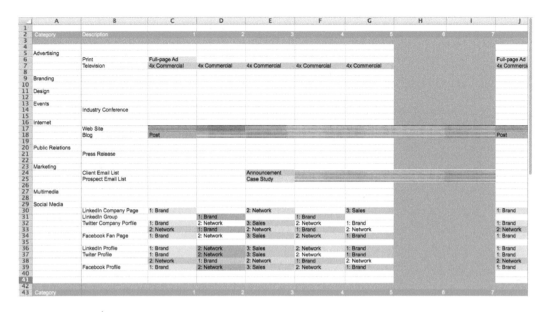

With the opportunities for outbound communication identified, so are the opportunities for engagement. Monitoring the activity in the network, responding to incoming messages, and managing the activity between people in the audience will demonstrate participation in social media. Without engagement, social media becomes just another broadcast tool speaking at people, not with them.

Each type of social media will have unique and appropriate responses to the message and the content. Many of the social media networks will demonstrate profile activity to other people within the network, like time stamps of posts and comments, or report new connections. Accounting for the "community activity" now includes the task in the deliverables, in the estimates of the required level of involvement, and in the evaluation of the model.

Models

At this point, the COMM Plan process has generated:

- Strategic thinking toward the weekly communication with an audience
- An executable to-do list to manage
- A "process model"—a representation of the communications process, before any actions are taken

This process model helps identify and understand each of the parts, learn what controls what, and discover how they interact with one another to complete a task or reach a goal. It allows us to understand how things work now and what would have to happen for the process to work differently in the future.

When a successful model has been proven, a business can move forward confidently, mitigating risk and managing investment. The business will also know what is relevant to measure over time, providing ongoing feedback on the model, which continually updates and improves the process.

Alternate Models

There's more than one way to communicate with an audience and hundreds of variables within that can make one model different than another. Varying messages, like headlines or offers in traditional A/B testing, can provide great insight into what messages resonate best with specific people on a small scale before expanding to a larger audience. Monday or Friday, morning or evening, picture or video, funny or serious—all variables to test and monitor in alternate models to learn what works and what works better.

Alternate models can be tested by applying a model to each week throughout the month or by assigning one model to the first half (two weeks) of the month, and the other to the second (two weeks). Although each model is unique, patterns and processes will reveal themselves over time. Extending the testing to a longer period provides even more data and feedback to make informed decisions on the construct of the model.

Weekly to Monthly to Annual

Each weekly model becomes the foundation for the month. Each monthly model becomes the basis for the year. Figure out the weekly approach and you have a proven model to build out the foundation of an annual communications plan.

Once completed, the COMM Plan will provide the strategic thinking toward communication, an executable to-do list to manage, and the criteria for benchmarks and measurement.

Invest the time now to develop a well-thought-out communications plan and you'll gain a perspective in the future that improves not only what you say, but how you say it—and in communications, isn't that what it's all about?

EXERCISE: Develop a Communications Plan Based on Goals

Every company communicates better with a plan. And although this may be easier for the experienced, it's crucial for every business, and in the long run it saves time and money.

1. Download the Communications Planning Template from the book website, or create a document based on the example provided. Account for each day of the month, denoting weekends, holidays, and special events.

2. Add each of the Social Media profiles to the communications plan on a unique line item to designate activity on each. Denote company profiles for the business, and personnel profile that will support your plan.

3. Add each of the other channels of communications available now and those that will

be available in each month. Denote the daily availability of a channel, like a website or social media. Denote the availability of a unique channel or content, like a blog post or press release, to provide an understanding of what is in play, current messaging, content available, and opportunities.

4. Develop a model for communications based on goals for the month. Address the indirect and direct communications opportunities.
- Select days to communicate (weekdays, per platform)
- Determine the number of messages per day / per week (per platform)
- Map goals to messages / adjust as necessary / variety
- Apply weekly model to other weeks (create month)

5. Develop the types of communications (a, b, c, etc.) and assign to each cell in the plan. Use the content types to create an editorial calendar that supports each goal for your audience. Integrate other channels of communications to best support each goal.

6. Develop the content strategy (per requirements), addressing the types of content (per goal). Detail options available for each. Review available content to repurpose / amortize investment in development. Test A, B, and C types of content providing a better understanding of what is working over time.

> ***Guarantee:** I guarantee that if you do everything I have taught you will generate a successful communications plan. - kp

Resources:

Download a template to develop a Comm Plan from the book website.

References:

Belch, George E., & Belch, Michael A. (2003). *Advertising and Promotion: An Integrated Marketing Communications Perspective: Sixth Edition.* Texas: McGraw-Hill. Retrieved from: http://www.slideshare.net/meerodeepo/mc-graw-hill-advertising-and-promotion-integrated-marketing-communication-20424624
Integrated Marketing Communications Definition. (2013). *American Marketing*

Association. Retrieved from: https://www.ama.org/resources/Pages/Dictionary. aspx?dLetter=I

Nielsen Newswire. Under the Influence: Consumer Trust in Advertising. Retrieved from: http://www.nielsen.com/us/en/insights/news/2013/under-the-influence-consumer-trust-in-advertising.html

Popovic, K. (2014, February 17). Planning How Your Business Communicates with Your Target Markets | Ideahaus®. Retrieved November 22, 2014, from http://ideahaus.com /2014/02/17/11425/

The University of Texas Division of Diversity and Community Engagement. *Strategic Planning Communications Plan.* Retrieved from: http://ddce.utexas.edu/2016/2010/07/strategic-planning-communications-plan/

The University of Texas Division of Diversity and Community Engagement. *Strategically Speaking.* Retrieved from: http://ddce.utexas.edu/2016/category/strategically-speaking/

West Virginia University. What Is IMC? Retrieved from: http://imc.wvu.edu/about/what_ is_imc

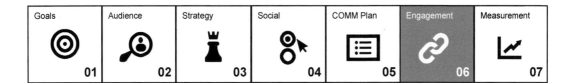

STEP 6

Creating Engagement

The appeal of social media to business has always been the invitation to "join the conversation." People are already talking about what you're selling—somewhere—and they may want to learn more, but most businesses don't understand that "join the conversation" does not mean "sell me your products and services." It means there is a current conversation in progress, and you're welcome to participate—just like in a real-world conversation between different people—but mind your manners.

Bad manners, blatant intrusions, and inappropriate language are not acceptable in public, in a restaurant, or in a place of business, and are surely not acceptable on social media.

You come to social media with business goals. People come to social media seeking engagement. The challenge is mapping business goals to the types of engagement to which your audience will positively respond (i.e., in a way that completes your activities and helps you reach your goals).

To engage users in a social network means to attract the audience you seek, to draw them into a conversation, and to hold their attention over a period of time. This definition also serves as the foundation of an ongoing social media strategy.

> *If my friend was trying to figure out how to get people to interact with them on social media, I would use a series of dating analogies. Depending on the gender, I'd use different examples, but all would be things where they know already what to do and what not to do. Think about your dating successes and disasters. Keep them in mind when you're trying to figure out if something is cool or if something is not. - kp*

Attracting an Audience

The social media profile presents a visual representation of you (or your business), but your content, behavior, and conversation are your substance. The words you share become your voice, the pictures you show become your face, and the way you interact with others—if you interact with others—becomes your visible personality. This, altogether, is the social media version of you and constitutes what you're offering to your target markets.

Draw Them into a Conversation

Sharing the right content and asking the right questions can start a conversation. Doing so over time keeps demonstrating who you are to your audience and what they can expect from a conversation. Because social communication goes both ways, it's important for a business to manage the conversation. A business needs to be there when something is said (monitoring) and answer, in a timely fashion, when a question is asked (response). This socially expected behavior is required to engage the audience in a way that keeps the discussion active. Acknowledge the people who are your contributors, manage their comments, and facilitate your conversations with them to serve your goals.

Hold Attention Over Time

Holding their attention over a period of time is dependent upon the amount of time required relative to your business goals. The type of product or service your company provides and the strength of your brand really dictates if people come and go (Like Snuggies—the blanket with sleeves. Remember?) or if they participate with your brand over time, like Coca-Cola (everybody knows Coca-Cola). Like any audience, you will gain new people and you'll lose some, but you'll always want to gain volume—and you need to if you ever expect to create real (statistical) engagement.

Following My Lead

With my first goal completed (create social media profiles that perpetuate my branding), I next needed to build my social network from the users of each social media. I needed to engage. Note that my strategy includes (personnel) pages for me and profiles for my business.

I started building my profile and professional network within LinkedIn because the demographics and psychographics of the media were a match for my target market—"an audience of Decision Makers (CEOs, CMOs, VPs)." It is also the most utilized business-class social network by the C-Suite (1). I would also be able to connect to Influencers (Directors, Managers) and Referrals (Staff, Consultants) that could also contribute to my goals.

In business, every professional is on LinkedIn, and it's become a question of "why?" if you are not. Answers may be, "they're too old," "they don't get it," "they're not that kind of businessperson." None of these are good. The first thing I do when I meet someone is check them out on LinkedIn. I bring some level of expectation based on my impression, so it's on the person to sway their perception. When I see more than I expect, I'm impressed. When I see less than I expect, I am unimpressed. I have been downright disillusioned by some because of the lack of effort and information some "professionals" put into their professional presentation. Naturally, it made me think less of them and their capacities—but that's me. - kp

After LinkedIn helped me connect with some of the people I already knew (high school, college, associations, etc.) from the data I included in my profile, it was time to start creating my audience. I used the LinkedIn advanced search to find CEOs within a 100-mile radius of Pittsburgh and San Diego, cities where my agency has studios and where we could easily meet in person. It came back with hundreds of people. I selected the profiles that had pictures of CEOs that I could see myself working with, that had good business experience, and that worked for companies that looked like they were doing well: in that order.

Their pictures said a thousand words, as advertised, and served as a first-level filter (just like a dating site). Experience in a market over time, the amount of education, and the geographic expanse of it all helps identify the experienced and knowledgeable—historically a better fit for our agency. Their successful company is indicative of revenue reinvested back into communications.

I sent them a message to connect that simply said:

> "Hi, Tom. My name is Kevin Popovic, and I'm the Communications Director of Ideahaus. For 30 years, I've helped businesses build brands and increase sales. Sometimes it helps to have a second opinion when making decisions for your company. Please consider adding me to your network as a resource. - kp"

Much like I'd introduce myself at a business mixer, I put out my hand, introduced myself, and let them know who I am and how I can help. What does society and our social graces direct us to do when we properly introduce ourselves and demonstrate value? You shake my hand and say, "Nice to meet you." Well, at least 70% of them did over time.

Seven out of every 10 accepted my request to connect, and the three that didn't are not active on LinkedIn (despite the profile) or just weren't that into me—which is fine. This filtering works both ways and complements our process to provide us with an audience.

The first engagement immediately followed notification of the new connection. Why? Because this is when you set the expectations with the other person. My goals require me to be able to speak with these people, so I set the tone and start the conversation in a message with a subject that gets them to read my message. Again, I go with simple and with something that I think will create interest (getting them to open the message is critical).

> Subject: Nice…
> Nice to connect, Tom – what are you working on today? – kp

Seriously, that's it. I've just got this person to connect with me. I want them to know I'm friendly and that I'm interested in learning more, just like they would experience if we were waiting for drinks at the bar. The headline approach is a touch of direct mail strategy: creating interest by using the unexpected. (Nice? Nice what? I'll open the message and read to find out.) This is also another filter; are they going to like my business personality?

Eight out of 10 respond over time. The two that don't aren't active on LinkedIn or they're just not that into me. The exercise (are you active) and the message (can you work with this type of person) continue to refine my audience to the people I need to reach my final goal: Use the social network to generate leads that turn into clients.

Understanding Process

The academic in me is a driven to understand these processes for improvement. Often, the better we represent a theory, the easier it becomes to understand how the pieces come together. For understanding engagement, I present this formula for consideration:

Formula for Social Engagement

$$\frac{(Perception)+(Content)+(Activity)}{(Connections)+(Time)} = Engagement$$

The perception generated by a social media profile plus the impact of the content shared and the activity displayed to a person over time is how you will impact your engagement using social networks. Your experiences plus measurement data and analysis will identify opportunities to improve your engagement strategy as you progress and you will start to identify trends (what works, what doesn't) with types of users in your audience.

Seven Types of Social Media Users*

Understanding the types of social media users in your audience will help you understand why people do what they do, why they don't do other things, and how you can work with them to help reach your goals.

In *Marketing in the Groundswell* (Li & Bernoff, 2009), Forrester Research suggested that there are seven types of social media users:

1. **Creator:** A person who publishes web pages, writes blogs, or uploads pictures or video to sites.
2. **Conversationalists:** A person who shares their thoughts and participates in a meaningful discussion.
3. **Critic:** A person who adds comments or who issues ratings and reviews.
4. **Collector:** A person who uses RSS and links to gather information and media.
5. **Joiner:** A person who uses multiple social networking sites.
6. **Spectator:** A person who reads blogs, looks at pictures, watches videos, listens to podcasts, etc. (a consumer of user-generated content).
7. **Inactive:** A person who has a profile but does not participate.

Seven Types of Social Media Users—Evaluation Rubric

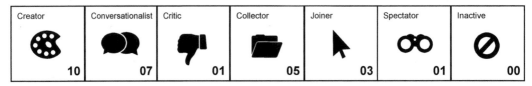

Creator	Conversationalist	Critic	Collector	Joiner	Spectator	Inactive
10	07	01	05	03	01	00

In this rubric, I assigned numeric values as I may value the different types of people in my own social media network. You can assign values, as you see fit, to help evaluate those in your network.

These categorizations can start to give you a better understanding of the types of people you're going to encounter in your audience, but nothing provides insight like seeing them for yourself.

Lurk and Learn

The best advice I've ever heard anyone give to someone getting started using social media to build positive engagement for their business is to "lurk and learn."

It sounds a little creepy, but "lurk" is a slang term used on social networks for people who have an account but don't actively participate. They read messages, status updates, and blog posts. They click on links, look at pictures, and watch video clips, but they're silent, seldom if ever updating their status or contributing to the public conversation. Some people choose to engage with social networking only by lurking, but that's not going to bring you closer to achieving your goals. Instead, what we want is a targeted, well-defined, and purposeful period of lurking, during which you have certain information to collect and objectives to achieve.

What You Will Learn

It may not seem like you're actually doing anything, but this is a period of ethnographic observation and a chance for your experiential assessment of the environment. It's also an opportunity to identify and gather the business intelligence you'll need to succeed.

In an article in *Harvard Business Review*, Ken Anderson suggests this type of ethnographic research can be "central to gaining a full understanding of your customers and the business itself," and I agree. Anderson goes on to say:

"Ethnography is the branch of anthropology that involves trying to understand how people live their lives. Unlike traditional market researchers, who ask specific, highly practical questions, anthropological researchers visit consumers in their homes or offices to observe and listen in a non-directed way. Our goal is to see people's behavior on their terms, not ours. While this observational method may appear inefficient, it enlightens us about the context in which customers would use a new product and the meaning that product might hold in their lives."

With eyes wide open, you should learn a great deal, including the following:

How Things Work

Pragmatic, and perhaps a bit boring, the learning period can be used to figure out exactly how each social media network functions. Watch the welcome video, take the tutorial, read the FAQs, visit the Help Center. Every functional thing you need to know is readily available.

Just as important: Take this time to watch other people. Watch what they say, how they share messages, how they upload photos, and what they include when they share links. Pay attention to if and when others respond, to which content and behaviors, and the interaction between the two (or more). These examples of a community in action should provide valuable insight when making your statements and responses.

Rules and Norms

Every service has its own TOS: Terms of Service. It's the large block of text most people never read providing the rules of the road. Violate the terms therein, and the service may take issue, disable your access, or bar you from participation entirely. Different ramifications may result if you're participating as a business.

Generally, complying with the TOS is no big deal. The harder part is identifying and complying with the unspoken rules and norms of the community, the self-policing social code of "how we do things here."

Pay attention to how members engage with each other, and pay special attention to negative examples. Members who get called out as *trolls* (a common term used on blogging platforms for commenters who are intentionally obnoxious, argumentative, or obscene) provide a great example of what *not* to do.

The only way to learn what these rules and norms are is to observe. Like travel and cultural experiences, you can read about them in a book, but it's different when you've been there. It's even more different if you've lived there for some time (as a local). The same incremental understanding occurs in social media.

Language Use

You can tell a lot about a person and what they think about their social media audience from the way they communicate in their space. Observing their style of language between the different types of people (Creator, Conversationalist, Critic) and how those different types choose to engage with each other can demonstrate where your opportunities to engage may be and where they may not be.

Type of Information Shared

People share content they think is of interest to their audience or that reflects some part of them. Pay attention to the types of information that different types of people share. This will help you discover what type of content the community is already consuming, what they find to be of value, and what they share (extending your reach) themselves.

Identifying High-Value Content

High-value content is content that users feel compelled to share with their friends and colleagues. The nature of social networking is such that most people have at least a few people in their circle who are not in the network where the user first encountered the content. So if the user wants their friends to see what they've liked, they pass it along.

Look for items that get retweeted on Twitter or updates/links on Facebook that many people like and share. It doesn't take long to get a sense of what's hot at the moment and what is getting the most attention over time.

How often do members update their status? How frequently do they share content? How many times is too much activity from just one person? It depends on the type of person.

A Creator, by nature, will share more content. A Conversationalist will respond as often as a Critic. A Collector, Joiner, or Spectator will just watch. The Inactive are, by definition, inactive.

Every social network will have a different answer based on the number of people it includes: Fewer people generate less conversation; more people generate more content.

Engagement between Members

How do people on the network initiate interaction? How do they engage with each other? How are businesses engaging with people? Does it work?

Look for examples of good and bad member engagements to understand boundaries between what is acceptable and what is not from the people in the network. You'll be joining these people, and you'll want to know what they expect.

Hello, My Name Is ...

Establishing a presence with people on social media is done just like you would when entering a social event, with a little bit of technology in between. Addressing this challenge in incremental steps, starting with the people you already know, makes the first few moments a lot less intimidating.

Internally

Leadership, management, and employees of your company are (statistically) already using social media and (statistically) have an interest in what their company is doing there. Establishing an initial audience with your own people will provide a sounding board for how the company is presenting itself to the public. From QA (quality assurance) to IMHO (in my humble opinion), your people will share their thoughts on what you're doing and how you're doing it. This feedback can be valuable—if you listen.

Make an announcement at work about the "soft opening" of a new social media profile—it's open, but unofficially, and we're just trying some things out. Send an email with links to your social media profiles, one at a time to keep them focused. If you send them five links, they will only visit one or two, and you won't get feedback on three, four, or five. Invite everyone to like, follow, or subscribe, and a percentage will comply.

Some people will be actively supportive, others just curious, but (from my experience) many will not come. A lot of people like to keep work and personal separate, and that's okay. We're just looking to seed the audience with some people who are looking out for us and who are willing to lend a hand.

Externally

The people outside your company who already know you and who work with your company are next. Clients, customers, vendors, suppliers—invite them to visit your profile for a specific reason, and include a call to action that gets them to join your network immediately. It's another group of people who have a working relationship with you that is (statistically) using the same social media as your company. This group will also give you feedback and fact check, which is welcome as you prepare to go public (new people). I find that people who already know a business tend to be more kind and forgiving to errors and missteps than those who are not.

One of the ways to reach your external audiences is to integrate your social media into the business communications you already use to communicate with them. Your website can include icons of your social media, quickly identifying where to find your profiles and providing links to get them there easily. Your advertising can include social icons, a web address (Facebook Icon/Target), or a username (@FritoLay). Utilize events for building followers through marketing promotions (i.e., follow us for a chance to win). Vehicle graphics, product packaging, and services collateral—all of which already go to your customers—are the easiest places to help people who already know your company know you're there.

Starting a Conversation

Sharing the right content and asking the right questions are only part of what it takes to keep an audience interested and to keep new people joining. You also have to be prepared to answer questions posed to you. Being responsive to the audience makes the public welcome and will keep members by providing what they need.

It's important to identify and build relationships with engaged core members—the super users. These individuals can be key contributors and can help steer overall conversations in a beneficial direction. Driving that conversation allows you to make the most effective use of the environment, which in turn allows you to build an audience around your company.

Make it easy to engage your content. Include social media sharing buttons at the end of your content. This placement will serve as a call to action at the end of your content and encourage users to share with their network. Only include the links to the major properties within which you're active to focus the conversation where you can monitor, measure, and respond.

Transparency vs. Opacity: There's a term in social media—"transparency"—which means that you are presenting yourself authentically. You are who you say you are —and your intent is clear. - kp

When a business joins social media, the assumption by the (non-business) users—and your audience—is that it is for business reasons. Coming into social media with the goals you created, you know this is true. Why else would you be here? Picture it as a viewer watching a television commercial: They know the commercial is here to sell them something. They may not know what your business is doing here yet or how you're going to do it, but they know you're up to something.

So you don't have to tell them everything, but you do have to tell them something.

There's a difference between "transparency" and "opacity," and in most cases I find opacity to be the wiser choice. I think it's important to represent your business accurately, and I think it's good to let them know you are there for business, but they don't have to know everything you're doing. They don't have to know the business results of your activity—some businesses don't even show how many fans they have to other fans. The point here is to be cognizant of what the medium expects and to be wise enough to pick what's proper to share to achieve your goals.

Most importantly, listen.

Building an Audience

As you participate with the people in your network, you're going to generate engagement—a like, a share, a comment—and then someone will follow you or join your group. This will happen again and again as you post, comment, and share. Repeating this process again and again is how you will build your audience.

Building an audience will take time, but there are some things you can do to help it along. First, make it easy. Don't complicate the process by making them jump through hoops to participate, and don't penalize them by over-communicating after they join your network. Be sure to demonstrate what's in it for them from the beginning, then fulfill your part of the agreement. Teach them how they can participate, and acknowledge the ones who participate like you'd like the others to do. This positive reinforcement will bring forward those who are waiting to see what happens.

Creating Relationships

There's a difference between a social connection—a person you are connected to via a like or a friend's status or a professional connection—and a social relationship—a person you are connected to via meaning or purpose.

Brands, like the National Football League (NFL) or Mini Cooper, often have existing equity in their audience from other platforms and their experiences within. Creating a profile for these existing relationships extends their brand into additional channels.

Businesses that don't have existing relationships will have to work to grow more audience members to earn social relationships. They will have to demonstrate their part of the relationship, over time, with social actions and behaviors to generate a response from the user to earn the relationship. It is in the repetition of these well-received actions by the audience that they will develop relationships.

Building Social Capital

The term "social capital" is new to a lot of us, but the concept isn't.

We've grown up with friends that we could call up in a pinch and ask to watch your kids or cut your grass or borrow $20 until payday. And they do it. Why? Because you have history, a relationship, and you've earned the right to ask your friend to do what friends do. At work, you can ask certain co-workers to cover for you, to help out with a project, to lend a hand when they didn't have to—and they do. Why? Because they know what it's like, and you'd do it for them.

For myself, I start measuring the success of my social media efforts in the increase of my social capital. Defined by Nan Lin as "investment in social relations with expected returns in the marketplace," social capital is a qualitative value and in most cases abstract. The reason I put so much effort into it all? I expect returns in my marketplace. And I get it, in numerous ways: branding, public relations, media relations, market awareness, marketing, sales and referrals. Albeit varying amounts and hard to quantify when not formally tracked, I can recount examples, ad nauseam, of each.

Sociologist Pierre Bourdieu explained that social capital is used to demonstrate how people receive direct and indirect opportunities to places of power and position through the employment of their social connections (i.e., he knew a guy who knew a guy who owed him a favor…). Although not equally available to all (Edwards and Foley), it can be increased, and everyone can get something out of it.

Today, social media is helping people maintain the relationships they already have in between the "traditional" contact, such as a phone call or a meeting or a holiday card, with an "untraditional" or "social media" contact, such as a text message, a status update, or a "tweet." Sociologists call this "social reciprocity." We've called this "friendship" or "camaraderie" or just simply "doing the right thing," and most of us have been taught or have learned the value of it. I, myself, attribute my success and longevity, in large part, to my friends and family that chipped in for me when I needed a hand.

Social capital is one of the returns businesses receive from social media. The goodwill generated by sharing content, providing information, or serving as a resource is reciprocated with a like, comment, or share. Progressively, it's the commitment to follow or subscribe, then a referral or recommendation to another. With enough social capital, you can ask for whatever you want and, depending on who they are and their perception of your relationship, you can decide if they will grant you your request.

Sometimes you have to remind some people they have a balance due, but people usually don't put a price tag on it or think of it like money in the bank. So, I think what we should remember is that there are many forms of ROI in professional relationships we each have in our overlapping worlds.

For most, the challenge is cashing in. So, once you "feel" like you have some social capital, how do you turn it into something of worth?

Well, it first depends on your business goals. What are you looking to get? A phone call, an introduction or referrals, inquiries, media coverage, investors and sales? I think we'd agree that each has a different "cost" depending on what it is and "fair market value." So, before you "spin that wheel" and ask, make sure you know what you want, and be as specific as you can. If you want an introduction, give them a job title or industry and let them know what you're going to do once you get it. The more information you can share, the better your connection can evaluate the request.

And whom do you want to get it from? A personal friend, a neighbor down the street, a business vendor, the guy you see at the club? Do your best to be realistic about your relationships, too. You don't bother the salesman at the Rolls Royce dealership when you know damn well you don't have the money to buy one, so don't waste your capital asking them for something you both know you can't afford.

Like any bank, you must have the funds available to make a withdrawal. And like business, you must have the right type of relationship to attempt what you're trying to do.

From Audience to Community

Within social media, the words "audience" and "community" are often interchanged. An audience is the people you have gathered. The community is the people that interact with one another.

A community of people that participates in a dialog is much more engaged and open to the messages you need to share and the actions you need to complete to achieve your goals.

Think about the way you share content with your audience that invites a conversation. Ask questions and be prepared to respond to them in a timely manner. Ask questions of the people who are sharing content to acknowledge their contribution and to demonstrate that you do converse and you are responsive. Most importantly, say "thank you."

Respond to the private or direct messages—those not shown in public—that you receive on each channel to prove you're listening and accessible. Use your social "inbox" as another way to demonstrate your customer service. When the community mentions you off your profile (and on theirs), acknowledge them appropriately.

These are the types of actions that can help improve your social media engagement audience moving forward to create a community.

Monitor and Manage

A community never succeeds without leadership. You have to do your part, and then some, to maintain its growth and prosperity.

You have to monitor your presence on your social media profiles, as well as on others. From fans to anti-fans, you'll need to know what is being said about your company in order to manage the conversations about you. Early access to an issue can avert a social incident leading to more people knowing about the issue than need be. Providing information where none is available can prevent others from filling in the blanks. Identifying opportunities, before they even happen, provides a time to shine in front of your audience.

You have to know what's going on in order to manage your perception. Being attentive to your profile is a start, but listening can get a little help from technology and functionality. Simple listening tools, like Google Alerts, can provide daily reports of keywords and phrases to your inbox. Searching your #hashtags, including your competitors', can provide a broad range of intelligence. Private lists, like those on Twitter, can provide a poor man's dashboard for everything you need to monitor.

Sharing content is at the core of communications, but so is the need to manage your content. When you post a picture, be sure to think about whom you're sharing with (public or fans). When you share a video, what types of creative commons licensing do you assign—and why? If you host the content on one service, make sure it is viewable on your other services. Monitoring changes in functionality and services is also important.

Manage your communication on a regular basis, and be consistent. Your actions teach an audience what to expect. Most businesses monitor communications on a daily basis due to the expectation of immediacy on social media. Anything more than 24 hours, and we see the user lose interest or feel as if they were not dealing with people. Depending on your volume of communication, you may or may not be able to service users as you'd like, just make sure to set and meet expectations.

When something happens, and it will, you'll need to have someone on deck for managing a crisis. From a customer complaint to a disgruntled employee, at some time there will be a communications crisis. Having a plan in place, in advance, enables community managers to respond without having to address the situation on their own. An FAQs or social media policy and guidelines is an important tool for properly responding and contacting the crisis.

Summary

In building engagement, you're doing so with other people who are interested in the same things as you. Give them a reason, and they will engage.

EXERCISE: Build Engagement on your Social Media

- Lurk and learn about each social media network and its user behavior.
- Provide a report for the complete social media platform.
- Identify types of users on each network.
- Identify types of content on each network.
- Identify types of relationships on each network.
- Identify opportunities within each network that align with your business goals.
- Launch your social media profiles internally.
- Promote your social media profiles externally.
- Monitor the activity and manage the engagement that occurs. Document your activity to provide complete reporting for reference and data for decision making.

References:

Anderson, Ken. Ethnographic Research: A Key to Strategy. (2009). *Harvard Business Review.* Retrieved from: https://hbr.org/2009/03/ethnographic-research-a-key-to-strategy/ar/1

Li, C., & Bernoff, J. (2009). *Marketing in the Groundswell.* Boston, MA: Harvard Business Press.

What's the Social Technographics Profile of Your Customers? (n.d.). Retrieved November 8, 2014, from: http://empowered.forrester.com/tool_consumer.html

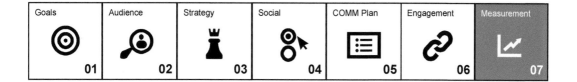

STEP 7

Measuring Performance

Depending on the Organization, "Performance" Can Mean Different Things.

If you work at Microsoft, you may have heard Bill Gates* say, "In business, the idea of measuring what you are doing, picking the measurements that count like customer satisfaction and performance ... you thrive on that."

If you worked at the White House, you may have heard former Secretary of Defense Donald Rumsfeld* state, "Your performance depends on your people. Select the best, train them and back them. When errors occur, give sharper guidance. If errors persist or if the fit feels wrong, help them move on. The country cannot afford amateur hour in the White House."

In a kinder, gentler world, Simon Sinek* suggests, "The world is a bell curve. Classroom test scores, employee performance in a company or how many people really, really like you. No matter the population you're studying, they always fit neatly across the standard deviations of the famous bell curve."

Literally, measuring performance is simply evaluating what we have done against the goals we've already defined, against the plan we put in place, to reach the audience we have defined, and using the metrics we've already agreed upon. It's the measurement of the manner in which the mechanism of our own design performs. But it's not just measuring the performance of content and technology, it's people, too, and how well we communicate. It's the measurement of the actions on both sides of the relationship and throughout the community. The human element is what makes this hard.

Figuratively, which is sometimes more succinct, it's telling a story about what we have accomplished. In defining "performance," I feel compelled to note that the most frequent references I had identified during my research had been those for "the performing arts"—in reference to a cast performing a play. I can't help but acknowledge the irony in the definitions.

Measuring performance can be the assessment by our audience of the performance on the stage of our creation—our social platform. Some may agree that, as Shakespeare so eloquently wrote in *As You Like It*, "All the world's a stage and all the men and women merely players." These actions we have choreographed—executing a well-written script to tell a story, connecting with the people in the audience—will keep them coming back for more and perhaps even evoke ... "Encore!"

No matter the influence of your definition, nor the manner in which your goals were established, this step of the process is about the measurement of performance, and the progress made toward reaching goals.

EXAMPLE

Measuring My Success

Personally, measuring the performance of my business will always mean measuring against my goals: quantitative or qualitative. I'm making an investment and I want a return. When I do not get one (I have learned), my business is impacted, most often for the worse. Each of the goals has been clear in direction, and each is measureable, so all I have to do is stick to the plan.

1. Create social media profiles for my business that perpetuate my existing branding.

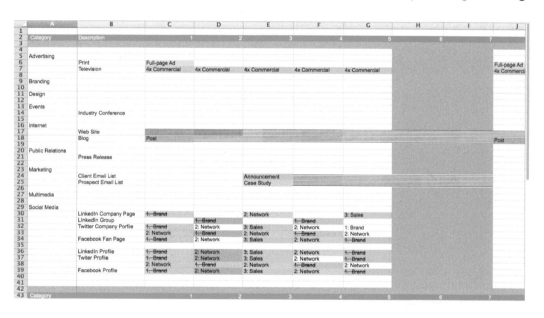

Measurement: My social media profiles had already been branded according to our guide-lines (pass). Over time, we're sharing content related to our brand across the social media platform and we're striking through each task when it gets completed (quantitative).

You can't measure this too much, but only measure what matters. - kp

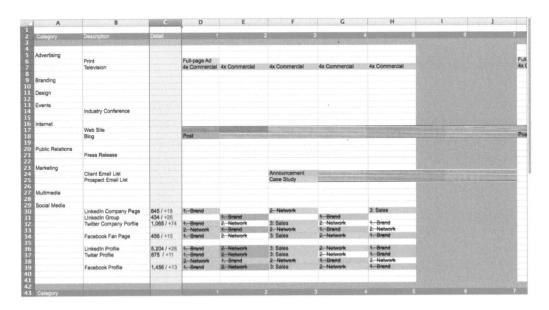

2. Build my social network from the users of select social media sites.

Measurement: Each task for the second goal is accounted for (2. Network), just like the first. Measuring the quantitative growth of my social network follows: Total how many people are in the audience at the end of every week, and report the plus or minus against the previous week to show progress.

The quantitative measurement of my performance across social channels is available from each network, at the source of the engagement:

• **LinkedIn Company Page** provides statistics on audience, updates, impressions, clicks, interactions, followers acquired, and engagement. Find graphs and reporting on reach, followers, visitors, demographics, and trends.

• **LinkedIn Group** provides statistics on members, seniority (by job role), comments, location, and function (position in their company). Look for further insight into demographics, growth, and activity.

• **Twitter** provides analytics for impressions, engagement (link clicks, retweets, favorites, replies) and engagement rates, per tweet, over a 28-day period. Follower analytics also provides data on interests, location, and gender.

• **Facebook Pages** provides extensive insights into page activity, including likes, reach, visits, posts, and people. Details of engagement reports growth, likes, comments, shares, and clicks, as well as post types, time of day, and location of engagement.

• **Facebook Profiles** provides a detail of activity on each profile, as well as the activity for the profile on other pages and profiles. For each activity, identify the number of likes and comments.

3. Use the social network to generate leads that turn into clients

Measurement: Measuring the qualitative will take more time because it requires an evaluation, but it provides even more valuable information regarding the progress of my actions. More is good, but better is better.

Social Network Evaluation Rubric

Referral	Influencer	Influencer +Budget	Decision Maker	Decision Maker +Budget
Re 01	**In** 03	**In^B** 05	**Dm** 07	**Dm^B** 10

Based on the established criteria in my Social Networking Evaluation Rubric, I evaluate the types of new people in the audience. Referring to the quantitative reporting, I know I have 318 new connections across my social platform. In evaluating the qualitative value of my connections, I learn some people have joined more than one network, providing specifically:

- 92: Referral within the company (92 pts)
- 115: Influencer within the company (345 pts)
- 13: Influencer within the company and has budget (65 pts)
- 41: Decision Maker within the company (287 pts)
- 28: Decision Maker within the company and has Budget (280 pts)

As of this measurement, the total value of this growth of my social network is 1,069 points, another data point in my ongoing measurement. Monitoring these people over time will provide the remaining information I need to measure the number of leads, those that become clients, and the dollars they invest in my company. Measurement will tell me how I'm doing and how far I have to go. Management will adjust my efforts, as needed, based on what I learn.

Measuring SMART Goals

As San Diego State Professor Steven Osinski* teaches, "Let the numbers be the task masters." Based on the SMART goals I established for my company, I can use the same data for evaluation against another methodology.

To review, my SMART goals included:

1. Specific: My company will invest to create a social media platform on Facebook, LinkedIn, and Twitter.
2. Measurable: We will share one message a day for three months to build an audience of 1,000 people for each social media network. The audience will consist of (50%) Decision Makers, (25%) Influencers, and (25%) Referrals.
3. Assignable: I am responsible for the direction of the content, my assistant is responsible for developing, posting according to a communications plan, and community engagement. We will both review the performance of each site twice a month and make corrections to the communications plan.
4. Realistic: We have set a goal of five new retainer clients generating $500,000 in new revenue.
5. Timely: We will repeat this process for 12 months and measure the value of the social media network, as well as report the revenue generated from new conversations from social media.

Depending on the level of evaluation, more or less data can be examined and reported, but in the end everyone just wants to know, "Did we reach our goals?" Five types of answers can be:

1. We did invest to create a social media platform on Facebook, LinkedIn and Twitter.
2. We did share one message a day for three months. We did build an audience of 1,000 people for Twitter (1,211), but not for the Facebook Fan Page (526) or the LinkedIn Company Profile (136). The audience consists of 23% Decision Makers (-27%), 42% Influencers (+27%), and 30% Referrals (+5%).
3. Each of the assignments was executed as prescribed. I directed the subject matter and content, my assistant curated and developed content and messages to share as scheduled. We reviewed each of the properties every two weeks to evaluate the performance, making changes to impact the growth of the audience. Some content performed better than others, and pictures were more engaged than videos. Twitter attracted the largest audience, while LinkedIn attracted the most Referrals, Influencers, and Decision Makers.
4. According to our CRM (Customer Relationship Manager) application, we developed three new retainer clients (-2) during the six months attributed to relationships initiated from social media. The revenue associated with these clients (during a six-month term) was $210,000 and is still active at the time of this publishing. To reach this goal requires two additional clients and $290,000 of revenue.

5. With two cycles completed, two more remain to fulfill the 12-month assignment. Measurement will continue, and adjustments will be made as we learn more.

Measuring Collaborative Goals

The development of our collaborative goals facilitated a conversation about our company and established a common understanding of the situation. The same data set applied to this type of goal structure provides an extension of that previous conversation and furthers the organization's understanding of the audience. A brief review of the goals provides context for the measurement (or skip right to the metrics to review the report).

History: Ideahaus was founded in 1990 as a creative communications agency. At the time, an agency that provided services in all channels of communication was viewed as over-reaching: Jack of all trades, master of none. Often compared to advertising agencies, design firms, or marketing groups, Ideahaus has maintained its focus. As additional channels have been added (Internet, Digital, Social Media, Mobile), Ideahaus has gained the knowledge and expertise to expand its service offering to clients.

Today: With the introduction and adoption of integrated marketing communications principles, the concept of an organization providing the spectrum of services has been more easily understood and embraced. The presentation of once-singular services (Advertising, Marketing, Public Relations, etc.) is now offered as more client-oriented services, including Communications Planning, Creative Development, and Account Management.

Vision: The opportunity for Ideahaus is to build a social media platform (LinkedIn, Twitter, Facebook) to share its insights, experiences, and samples of work with an audience of Referrals, Influencers, and Decision Makers that presents our company as thought leaders and subject matter experts. In presenting an expanse of information and content on each type of communications, we demonstrate our understanding of each. By presenting stories about our IMC approach to communications planning and examples of our creative development, we will demonstrate that we are a subject matter expert and a qualified resource.

Issues: Building an audience of people is different than building an audience of prospects. We need to attract more than just people; we need people in the job roles of the companies that would contract our agency.

Goals: Ideahaus needs to build a social media platform to share information and content that clarifies who we are, what we do, and whom we help.

Ideahaus needs to build a social media network with the types of people we want to work with and for. These types of people would need professional services in Communications Planning, Creative Development, and Account Management.

The people who work for Ideahaus must continue the conversations the company begins. People will interact with our company, and they can engage with our people. Our company must create interest and attract the right people. Our people must identify the types of people we attract and engage them appropriately.

The result of this activity will create new conversations with new people that turn into new business opportunities.

Metrics: Each of the (3) goals requires different actions and resources to complete, as well as different metrics for measurement.

Business and Personnel social media profiles have been branded according to our guidelines (completed). Over time, we're sharing content related to our brand (who we are, what we do, who we help) across the social media platform and measuring the delivery of each message (quantitative).

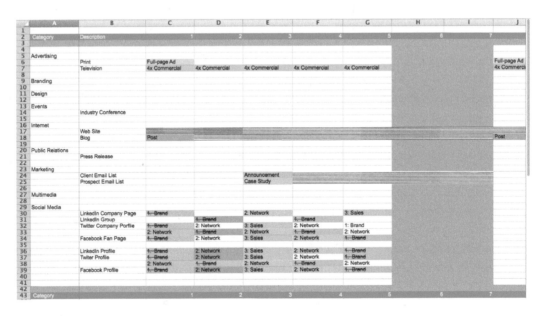

Category	Description	1	2	3	4	5	6	7
Advertising								
	Print	Full-page Ad						Full-page Ad
	Television	4x Commercial	4x Commercial	4x Commercial	4x Commercial	4x Commercial		4x Commercial
Branding								
Design								
Events								
	Industry Conference							
Internet								
	Web Site							
	Blog	Post						Post
Public Relations								
	Press Release							
Marketing								
	Client Email List			Announcement				
	Prospect Email List			Case Study				
Multimedia								
Social Media								
	LinkedIn Company Page	1: Brand		2: Network		3: Sales		
	LinkedIn Group		1: Brand		1: Brand			
	Twitter Company Porfile	1: Brand	2: Network	3: Sales	2: Network	1: Brand		
		2: Network	1: Brand	2: Network	1: Brand	2: Network		
	Facebook Fan Page	1: Brand	2: Network	3: Sales	2: Network	1: Brand		
	LinkedIn Profile	1: Brand	2: Network	3: Sales	2: Network	1: Brand		
	Twiter Profile	1: Brand	2: Network	3: Sales	2: Network	1: Brand		
		2: Network	1: Brand	2: Network	1: Brand	2: Network		
	Facebook Profile	1: Brand	2: Network	3: Sales	2: Network	1: Brand		
Category		1	2	3	4	5	6	7

Social media networks have been established (2. Network) and measured monthly to monitor the (quantitative) growth.

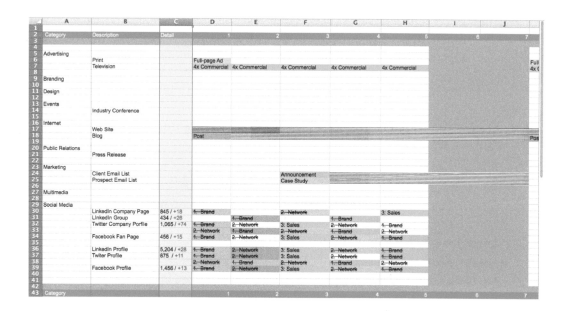

All data is recorded from the source of the engagement: LinkedIn, Twitter, Facebook. Based on the established criteria in the Social Networking Evaluation Rubric, all new connections are noted within our CRM (Customer Relationship Manager) and identified as Referrals, Influencers, or Decision Makers.

Social Network Evaluation Rubric

The total value of this growth of the social network is 1,069 points, another data point in the ongoing measurement. Monitoring these new conversations over time will measure the number of leads, those that become clients, and the new revenue generated from this investment.

Measure What Matters

No matter which process has been used to establish goals, each comes with a metric for measurement. For most, all of this will boil down to "How far have we come?" and "How far do we need to go?"

1. Measure the execution of the Communications Plan, then discuss:

- Are we executing against the plan on time, as planned?
- What percentage of actions is being executed as planned?
- Does it require the time (hours) your team had allocated to the budget?
- Does your team have the resources it needs to best execute the plan?
- Are all the types of content available, as required?
- Are the different types of channels integrating, as planned?
- Are there any additional channels that could be integrated in this plan?
- What could be done to improve the execution of the plan?
- Is the model performing as conceived?
- Are there any new opportunities identified?
- Are the messages being delivered, as designed?
- What could be done to improve the process model?
- How do the models compare to each other?

Based on the results of this measurement, prioritize the models being utilized. Adjust the budget and resources allocated to the communications plan for the following period.

The use of a CRM (Customer Relationship Manager) application will contribute to the successful management and nurturing of your relationships. With success comes scale, and there's no easy way to manage all of the old information for each person in your audience, let alone monitor all of the new interactions. Get savvy with the application your organization currently uses, or start shopping for the one you will use before somebody says, "Hey, we really need a CRM." - kp

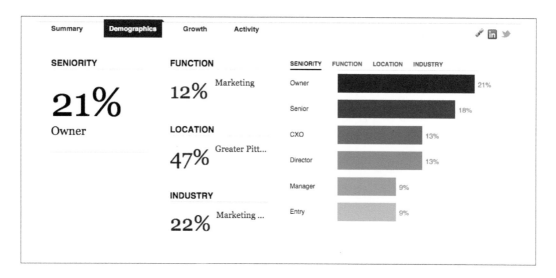

2. Measure the Engagement with the audience, then discuss:

- Are we attracting our target audience?
- Are we engaging them? How much and when? Where?
- What types of people are we attracting (of the seven types): Creator, Conversationalist, Critic, Collector, Joiner, Spectator, or Inactive.
- What are we learning from watching our audience?
- What have we learned about the way people interact with content?
- What have we learned about the way people interact with each other?
- What have we learned about the language people use?
- What type(s) of content are they sharing with us? With each other?
- How do they participate? How often do they participate?
- Are we increasing our social capital?
- Are we creating a community?

3. Review the Social Media selected to reach the target audience, then discuss:

- What have we learned about each social network?
- Have we established open channels of communication with our audience?
- What have we learned about content sharing?
- Where and how do people utilize the functionality?
- What have we learned about collaboration?
- Are personnel profiles supporting business profiles?
- How does this business compare to its competitors in the same network?

- Have all of the opportunities been realized in the presentation of the business to the target audience?
- Is all of the information about the business complete and accurate?
- Has the business maintained compliance with each social media network?
- Are the social media selected performing as expected?
- What properties should be reprioritized?
- Are there any new opportunities to better present the business to its audience or within the social media network?

4. Review the Strategy Overview, then discuss:

- Is the executed strategy supporting the company mission statement?
- Are you executing against your SWOT strategy?
- What is working? What is not?
- Have you identified new strengths, weaknesses, opportunities, or threats?
- How does this impact your current strategy?
- Are you prepared to make changes to your strategy?
- How is the content performing in support of the goals?
- What could you do to improve the content for your audience?
- Are you providing what they each want?
- What other types of content could you provide? What else is available?

5. Review the Audience being targeted, then discuss:

- Who did you target? Who did you attract?
- Do the people in your network match their User Profile?
- What have you learned about your audience that you did not know before?
- How accurate were your role-playing scenarios?
- Are people interacting with your properties like you thought they would?
- What will you have to do to differently in the future?

6. Measure the progress toward the established Goals, then discuss:

- Were you able to measure what you thought you could measure?
- Are you making progress toward the goals? Why or why not?
- Can you better define any of your goals today with your new information and experiences?
- Have you identified any new goals for consideration?
- Are you prepared to invest in additional goals at this time?

Each of these types of discussions about each of these specific steps will provide ongoing insight to those who execute, at a level where change comes quickly. The same measurement, viewed as a whole, provides that 10,000-foot view that is so important to maintain for management.

I remember the old line, "Plan the work, work the plan." I also know what it takes to do the administrative part of communications—often its more work that the message and content development. When we get busy, or budgets get tight, it's sometimes easy to rationalize shortcuts. Experience teaches me, "Don't take shortcuts." Do the work and the plan will work. Take a shortcut and expect less. - kp

EXERCISE: Measure Your Performance

1. Based on your goals, draft a document to measure your performance for each part of the process:

- Communications Plan
- Engagement
- Social Media
- Strategy
- Audience
- Goals

2. Add the criteria you had agreed upon in advance to each section. Follow the guidelines you established at the beginning.

3. Collect the quantitative and qualitative data, interpret, and report. Only report the data appropriate for each of the sections.

4. Discuss the results with your team.

5. Adjust accordingly.

6. Repeat weekly.

I told the old guys in my audience we can measure the progress and success of Satellite Marketing like the trajectory of a satellite we have launched into our market space against a trajectory: Is on course? Is it reporting data? Does it respond to our control? Over time, we'll look for signs of orbital decay and adjust its trajectory accordingly to keep it on track and communicating with mission control. Without the monitoring and ongoing adjustment, we cannot guarantee the satellite will perform as designed. For as much as we have planned, things change, so we adjust. - kp

References

Meyers, J. (2013, March 13). Bill Gates on D.C.: "You don't run a business like this." Retrieved November 12, 2014, from http://www.politico.com/story/2013/03/bill-gates-on-dc-you-dont-run-a-business-like-this-88830.html

Rumsfeld, D. (n.d.). BrainyQuote.com. Retrieved November 12, 2014, from BrainyQuote.com Website:http://www.brainyquote.com/quotes/quotes/d/donaldrums135926.html

Sinek, S. (n.d.). BrainyQuote.com. Retrieved November 12, 2014, from BrainyQuote.com Website: http://www.brainyquote.com/quotes/quotes/s/simonsinek568195.html

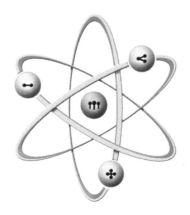

CHAPTER SIX

Business-to-Consumer Case Story: Stylin Online

Business-to-Consumer Case Story: Stylin Online

One of the first opportunities I had to really apply my theories of *Satellite Marketing* to a large-scale audience was for an online retailer based in Memphis, Michigan, that sold Teenage Mutant Ninja Turtles t-shirts. The company is called Stylin Online.

History: In 1995, with a loan from his grandfather, James Cucchiara founded Stylin Online and turned his childhood love of comics into having his own business. He used a favorite high school doodle as a logo, launched his website using Yahoo! E-commerce, and his business grew by leaps and bounds (just like in *Superman* Volume 1). Online sales grew from zero, and James began to sell licensed products directly to comic fans at local events and conventions across the country.

Stylin Online CEO James Cucchiara in The Tower of T-Shirts

Today: Stylin Online has become one of the biggest names in pop culture apparel and accessories, with over 200,000 SKUs of t-shirts, hoodies, hats, and everything else to which you can apply a licensed logo. From The A-Team to Zelda—and everything in between—Stylin Online sells something from everything you loved growing up as a kid.

Issue: Then the market changed, and sales faltered. Big retailers started carrying parody merchandise, and more vendors attended events. The economy dropped and took discretionary spending with it, a bad sign for a CEO who depended on the sale of superhero t-shirts and horror movie hoodies for his livelihood. Discount promotions kept Stylin Online alive, but the discounts cut into his profit margin.

At conferences and online, James commiserated with his colleagues who were experiencing similar challenges, and he kept hearing how they were looking to social media to change their business. He heard how he could connect with his fans, create brand loyalists, and revive company sales, but he had no idea where to start. He was an expert in apparel and in pop comic culture, not in social media. He needed help.

At the same time, I had just started teaching workshops on social media in San Diego. A mutual friend who attended one of my workshops recommended James contact me to see if something made sense. While at the wheel of a 40-foot-long RV and leading a three-truck caravan, James called me (not hands-free) and spent the next four hours discussing his business and his goals for social media, asking question after question of how I could help.

Vision: James told me, "We've built a good company with e-commerce, email, and events, but we don't know anything about social media. I don't have time to learn something new, and I don't have people in-house that can handle this. I want someone to tell me what I need to know, help me figure out what my company should do, and then take care of it."

I told him about our company and the story about using satellites as a metaphor for how people engage with social media. James got it, and with a simple "Sounds like a plan," he authorized one of our most successful working relationships.

1. Identifying the Goals

James told me his primary goal was to drive more targeted traffic to the website. Stylin Online had loyal customers who bought from them when they bought, but the company needed more new customers to maintain growth. James knew his site metrics (how well his website performed) and his visitor-to-purchase ratio (how many people it took to visit his site to generate X amount of revenue)—he just needed more people.

In the short term, we were charged with increasing the number of Facebook Fan Page fans. More fans would increase the number of opt-in prospects for our sales and marketing campaigns. A bigger fan base of brand-loyal shoppers would mean more people to whom we should market online purchases and more people that would know about the convention appearances (i.e., Stylin Online is coming to a convention near you!). The more Facebook fans we had, the more people would see our messages, and a predictable percentage would turn into customers (that's how it worked in 2009).

Our next goal was to build the brand. Honestly, you can find a Spiderman t-shirt anywhere —but why were fans going to buy a commodity product from Stylin Online? We had to give them a reason.

1. Increase traffic to the online store
    a. Traffic measured by Google Analytics (quantitative)
    b. Measure sources impacted by communications plan (monthly)
2. Build an audience on Facebook Fan Page
    a. Growth measured by Facebook (quantitative)
    b. Measure fan growth (monthly)
3. Build the Stylin Online brand
    a. Develop Integrated Marketing Communications
    b. Measure Positive Response (Qualitative)

2. Understanding the Audience

We surveyed current customers and Facebook fans regarding their attraction to the Stylin Online brand, the website, products, and the social media community. We identified various strategies that successful brands used to grow their Facebook fan base, including loyalty discounts, early access to exclusive products, and pictures of fans and celebrities from the conventions.

The target audience for Stylin Online is the fans of pop culture. Pop culture fans are interested, loyal, and zealous in their support of the actors, heroes, and intellectual property they have connected with. Fans also look for other fans to discuss the past, to share the new, and to convert those who have not come on board with what they believe is the obvious choice in a sea of entertainment.

These fans can be categorized as "die-hard" fans, the men and women (18–55) from across the United States who stand in line for tickets, who never miss an opening weekend and who can recount line after line from their favorite villain or superhero from every episode ever made. They commonly demonstrate their fandom in their fashion via t-shirts, sweatshirts, hats, and accessories, representing the very best of comics, television, movies, sci-fi, horror, anime, cartoons, Disney, video games, and music.

We learned that our products were well regarded across niche communities, and throughout every convention. Online fan testimonials, celebrity attraction, and media coverage demonstrated an interest in the brand and its 200,000-SKU inventory.

3. Creating the Strategy

Managed from an ever-expanding warehouse, Stylin Online retails their products at more than 50 annual fan and comic conventions across the United States and abroad. With each mobile store measuring 20'x 40' and 20' high, we dubbed each a "Tower of T-Shirts" and presented them collectively as "Your Pop Culture Department Store™"—a tangible destination.

We knew that one of Stylin Online's strengths had been their selection of products with repeat customers online and with event organizers on the convention circuit. Organizers had a vendor that provided what the fans were looking for, and their attendance at conventions each year had established Stylin Online as a must-have vendor. The expected relationships followed, and his social capital grew with convention organizers at every show. The question was, "How can we leverage this for our mutual gain?"

Each convention would also put the company in the same room with media personalities and celebrities, many of which shopped our store. We found we had access to an array of celebrity customers associated with many of the products in our inventory, and that they would be willing to discuss their roles and experiences behind the scenes and during the making of their TV show, movie, or comic. We discussed our concepts with them and their managers to address: "How can we help promote your celebrity appearance?"

Our experience with sharing celebrity pictures had been positive throughout the social media platform and had now progressed to video "shout-outs" with great reactions from their respective fans. We started by sharing the photos from the warehouse, then photos from the conventions. Every so often, we'd get photos of James with a celebrity inside the Tower of T-Shirts from a show at which he sold merchandise. They'd hold up a t-shirt or put one on and smile for the camera, providing unique and original content on a regular basis.

We discussed our approach with the celebrity media with which we had developed relationships during award shows and celebrity gift suites in Hollywood (yes, *the* Hollywood, a long way from Memphis). They shared what they liked about videos, fans, and interviews as well as what they did not. Collectively, it was a wealth of information.

The strategy was to create a video marketing vehicle to activate the passion of a fan (attract their attention), provide new content (draw them into a discussion), and to encourage discussion (hold their attention over a period of time). This strategy would be designed to target not only current Stylin Online fans (increase the per-ticket sale), but to also gain exposure with those unaware of Stylin Online (i.e., new customers).

We decided to make *I am stylin' | Adventures in Pop Culture,* a web-based show featuring celebrity interviews, award show gift suites, comic conventions, and fan experiences. As a stand-alone media property sponsored by Stylin Online, the company was prominent on every episode, including branding, product placement, trial / implementation, and content development.

4. Selecting Social Media

We built a Facebook presence for Stylin Online: a fan page for the company, a personnel profile for James, and a unique Facebook event for each convention appearance. We built on the pilot from the Anaheim Comic Con, updated during the Motor City Comic Con, and fine-tuned for the San Diego Comic Con (the largest event of its type in the world). Our original distribution included the expected YouTube and Facebook, but as popularity grew, so did the popularity of other video networks, like Veoh, Vimeo, and MetaCafe. We identified an opportunity to reduce our time to market with a distribution network, a single source that would distribute to multiple video sites.

To build the audience for the show, we took the show to where the audience was already watching videos just like ours.

Uploading to YouTube took the same time as it did to upload to Blip.tv—it just sent it out to 21 sites. The distribution network was also expanded to (35) satellites utilizing video services, blogs, and social media including:

- AOL Video
- Blinkx
- iamstylin
- StylinOnline
- Boxee
- Daily Motion
- DivX TV
- eBaums World
- Facebook
- MetaCafe

- Mefeedia
- GrindTV
- Internet Archive
- iTunes
- Twitter
- Sony BVL
- StupidVideos
- Yahoo Video
- Roku
- Samsung

- Sevenload
- Twitter
- Veoh
- VideoJug
- Vimeo
- Vizio
- Vodpod
- YouTube
- Zoopy

5. Building Engagement

Commercials at the end of an episode and text included in the video description were perceived as valuable to the sponsor, but front and center above the "show more" and always visible to a visitor was the "Sponsored by http://StylinOnline.com—Watch this episode for a promo code!"

The description copy also evolved to include a link to those we interviewed. It was a courtesy to those who took the time—a way for their fans to learn more—and a demonstration of the types of things we did for those who would grant us an interview in the future. They participate in our program, and we promote them to our growing audience. The quid pro quo was demonstrated, which made the opportunities come easier.

Following the debut of the San Diego Comic Con episodes, the show was granted media credentials to every event. This increased the credibility of the show and provided additional access and information previously unavailable (hype begets hype).

We posted videos, fans made comments. We asked questions, fans offered answers and opinions. When we posted the interview list in advance, we collected questions fans wanted to ask—and we used their questions to conduct the interview. We gave the question and the fan's name to the celebrity and let them answer directly.

This "Content Marketing" from the conventions and events provided various media to initiate conversations, to share content, and to collaborate on the events our audience is interested in discussing. This quid pro quo over time helped develop the brand, its social capital, and more importantly, the ongoing customer relationship.

With simple email marketing to his customer list, we quickly grew the Facebook Fan Page to 1,000, then 2,000 and then up to 5,000!

Then we hit a wall.

For every 100 qualified contacts Stylin Online gained, they lost another 100. Five-thousand fluctuating fans wasn't going to change his sales. In a candid conversation with me, James said, "If you guys can't move the needle any farther, then I can't justify the investment." We were going to lose this account, and James would be no better off than when he had first called.

I went back to my team and asked the hard question: "What are we doing wrong?" With a customer list of 125,000 emails and 500 million people on Facebook (at the time), we had to do better than 5,000 fans. We're the experts; how could we fix this? Then it hit me! We made a classic marketing mistake: We set the wrong goal! James didn't need "likes" on his Facebook page. He needed to find Facebook users who were interested in buying his products.

6. Communications Planning

The model for weekly communication had evolved over time to accommodate the wide range of fans in the audience. Each category was represented (comics, television, movies, sci-fi, horror, anime, cartoons, Disney, video games, and music), and fans reacted when they were provided content that appealed to their particular interest. The weekly model provided the foundation for the monthly, and the monthly for the year in advance.

We also developed a model for conventions that included pre-event, event, and post-event marketing. We contacted celebrities in advance to coordinate public relations opportunities, exchange social media pleasantries, and plan the pre-production of the show. As a new convention was added to the calendar, the model was applied to the communications plan.

We had a great plan for engagement; we just needed more people to engage.

We identified Facebook Advertising as an additional channel for attracting new Facebook Fans. With the ability to target demographics (age, gender) and areas of self-declared interest (comics, television, movies, sci-fi, horror, anime, cartoons, Disney, video games, and music), we knew we could isolate the prospects for subject-specific messaging and effectively present the case for why they should "like" Stylin Online.

We invested $100 to test a Facebook ad campaign that targeted two of the largest niche customers: Marvel and DC Comics. The ads were basic, using the title from the fan page name as its headline (Stylin Online). They included a 110 x 80-pixel image and 135 characters of text. The opportunity for creativity was limited to the 100-or-so characters of text, including a simple offer: "Like our page to connect with other fans, just like you."

7. Measuring Performance

The 200,000-SKU product inventory provided a seemingly endless library of licensed imagery—a visual sample of the product line Stylin Online had available for each fan. The license to sell the shirts allowed us to use the product in its promotion. Although the thumbnails were small, the images of superhero emblems and character sketches greatly resonated with fans, and clicks started coming faster than we could track them. New fans literally came with every browser refresh, peaking one day at 10,000 new fans!

We employed common "best practices" for advertising strategy (get their attention, get them to do something) and A/B tested countless versions of ad copy and images. The activity of the campaign was monitored directly within Facebook, reporting reach, frequency, impressions, click-thru rates, and budgets for the bidding.

Side Note: A/B testing is a simple method for testing which of two ads performs better: A or B? Two identical ads, except for one element: The picture, the headline, or the call-to-action—but just one thing at a time. Run the two ads to the same sample size and compare the results; one usually performs better. Take that performing ad and change one element, then run two ads again. This constant testing and refinement will provide ads that work and the data to prove the ROI (or lack thereof). - kp

Once we identified the strategy that worked both for the specific medium of Facebook ads and for our specific fan base, we invested heavily in running concurrent campaigns, monitoring and adjusting bid rates accordingly. Each ad generated a different bid range although they shared a common daily budget. As an ad's performance declined, a new ad was released to replace it. Cost per clicks (likes) ranged as much as $0.42 and as low as $0.04 per new fan.

More clicks increased our investment, and our investments kept showing a return. 10,000 fans. 50,000 fans. 100,000 fans! After investing just over $6,000, Stylin Online had more than 200,000 Facebook fans from all over the world—and they were all buying our product!

From the Quantitative...

Over 18-months we produced 180 episodes of *I am stylin / Adventures in Pop Culture* with an average program length of 6 minutes. Each episode includes a link to the online store, links to the show's website, and product(s) included in the episode. These links multiplied by the total number of distribution points has made a dramatic impact on the SEO (Search Engine Optimization) the client receives in Google, etc.

We learned that the longer the video the fewer people viewed the entire show. As expected, total views of each episode was a monitored metric, ranging from hundreds to thousands per social media profile (times 35 profiles), depending on the subject matter and quality of the interview. Actor Jon Bernthal from *The Walking Dead* on AMC answering fan questions from the Stylin Online Facebook Fan page was a crowd favorite on the show from Chicago's C2E2 Convention on the I am stylin YouTube channel, while Academy Award-nominated actor Edward James Olmos from Atlanta's DragonCon did not perform well on DailyMotion (but did on other sites). The total views were indicative of how well coupon codes inside each episode would be redeemed (10% off next order, free shipping, etc.): More views, more redemptions during a sale.

Stylin Online became a brand, and "I am stylin" was a ticket into anywhere in pop culture. People wanted to be on our show, and our audience wanted to watch. The resulting impact of the client's SEO (Search Engine Optimization) was dramatic to say the least. Thirty-five websites across the Internet using matching keywords and sharing a single link helped get Stylin Online in front of other advertisers for the same products (they're a retailer, not a wholesaler) and delivered new customers.

Now, every producer secretly hopes his or her efforts will become a million-view Internet sensation, but we were more pragmatic about the opportunity, especially over time. We

Side Note: For stories like this to happen, you need to have a team that is motivated to move the needle and a client who is prepared to invest. You can't scale down effort from either parts and expect success. - kp

considered the number of videos on the number of sites, with the number of views, and the number of visits to the website from a video. We also considered that these resources would be available online, and in any search, until we took them down or they were removed.

We started the Stylin Online fan page with just under 5,500 fans July 1, 2010, and exceeded 225,000 by December 1, 2010, an increase of just under 220,000 new fans in only 5 months. The Facebook Fan Page has become the third largest source of traffic for StylinOnline.com, after Google search and the direct URL.*

From the Qualitative...

In less than two years, we repackaged the company and established the Stylin Online brand as "Your Pop Culture Department Store" and as a leader in the pop culture retail industry. As William Shatner said after landing his helicopter on the deck of the USS Midway en route to the San Diego Comic Con, "Mission Accomplished."

References

Statistics provided by Facebook Insights and Google Analytics over the period reported. Links to videos, as retrieved 9-25-2014.

Video retrieved from https://www.youtube.com/user/iamstylin

Stylin Online Facebook Fan page, as retrieved 9-25-2014: https://www.facebook.com/ Stylin-Online-103484575747/

"Moving the needle doesn't just happen. Somebody executed a well-thought-out plan."

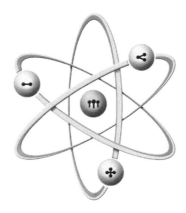

CHAPTER SEVEN

Business-to-Business Case Story: Bokwa Fitness

Business-to-Business Case Story: Bokwa Fitness

Bokwa® is a group fitness program developed by international fitness personality Paul Mavi, a leading Los Angeles-based Group Fitness Instructor. Tapping into his native South African roots as a dancer and musician, Paul developed Bokwa for his own classes over an 8-year period. Within a Bokwa class, participants draw letters and numbers with their feet, while moving together to music in free form rhythm. From 4-year-old kids, to men and women in their seventies, to guys with "2 left feet," to world champion dancers, Bokwa engages participants of all ages in the same class and to the same music.

In early 2012, Paul partnered with a seasoned direct response television and fitness entrepreneur to grow the business internationally. Since then, Bokwa has developed a loyal following across the globe with certified instructors and participants in dozens of countries. The Bokwa Fitness business model offers certifications to Independent Group Fitness Instructors who are offering Bokwa classes to students in some of the largest health club chains, independent studios, schools, and community centers.

History: Bokwa Fitness became very popular very fast in Los Angeles. The program was an alternative to other music-based programs, like Zumba®, and offered a wider selection of music (not just one genre). The instruction was also intuitive to anyone who knew the alphabet so adoption and retention was greater than programs where a new language or choreography was required.

Today: Paul and his partner had Bokwa well positioned for an accelerated development cycle. Bokwa would certify instructors by teaching them the program and generate revenue from certifications. The instructors would teach students in their own classes to generate their revenue. Between Bokwa and the instructors, they would generate interest and demand in the program.

Paul was a personality with personality, and his enthusiasm with the program came shining through. His partner came from a direct-to-consumer background and had been very success- ful with taking products to market internationally. These were some of the big draws for the instructors who had taken Bokwa in Los Angeles—experience and excitement—what both were trying to leverage to grow the business.

The following Bokwa was able to generate in Los Angeles demonstrated the program was successful, and the interest of the instructors that took the classes and wanted to teach their students Bokwa showed there was an opportunity to grow.

The question was, "How?"

Vision: Paul already had a following in Los Angeles, and a number of his students were international: some from the United Kingdom, some from Australia, and some even from Taiwan. They had shared Bokwa with their friends and colleagues, and that was a great start in the United States, but the real opportunity was to build the business outside the United States. There are more people outside the United States than inside, and if the business was going to be successful—really successful—then it needed to have as many people interested, from as many places, as possible.

The vision was to take what has worked in Los Angeles and introduce it to the world.

Issues: There are two audiences for Bokwa (the company): instructors and students; instructors, because that was the source of revenue for the company (the paid classes and certifications), and students who were interested in taking Bokwa classes from the Certified Instructors. If the latter didn't come, the former would not renew their certifications.

Bokwa would have to build their brand to create a demand for the certifications while creating awareness and demand for the program.

Promoting the program in Los Angeles was easy: Paul and his team had been in the business for years, they knew the who's who in the market, and knew how to grow a local following using word-of-mouth and personal recommendations. Promoting the program internationally would take more people, more organization, and require communications channels to the instructors, their students, and prospects (people who had not ever heard of Bokwa). His partner had been successful with using paid media in the past (direct-to-con- sumer television) but to achieve the exposure they required with TV would be cost-prohib- itive: just too much money.

This is where we joined the team. His partner wanted to know if we could use social media to replace television, and I said, "it depends on your goals."

1. Identifying the Goals

When I met with Bokwa, we discussed the issues they were having with preparing to launch the business internationally. They had the program, they had the certifications, they had early adopting instructors, and they had a list of goals they needed to address. What they needed were answers to the following questions:

• How could they build the Bokwa™ brand and promote the Bokwa program?
• How could they identify and certify instructors that could build a following for Bokwa?
• How could they attract students to the Bokwa program and help them find an instructor?

2. Understanding the Audience

The instructors, as an audience, are high-energy people who make a living off of their passion for fitness and exercise. Their knowledge and energy get them in shape, while their contagious enthusiasm and leadership is what their students pay for. Most instructors were female (80%–90%) and younger than older (20–35 years old).

The students are a mixed bunch: some are people who are as energetic as the instructors and keep pace every class. Some don't have as much time to commit but work to include it as part of their life. Others, the largest market, workout every so often and wish they did more. They don't participate in a fitness program because it doesn't fit into their schedule, or the programs they have tried are too complicated and require coordination they don't think they have. Demographics showed women were the majority (75%–90%) of the market potential, and the age range for potential students of organized fitness programs were 18–65.

3. Creating the Strategy

Paul and his partner had a great start on building the Bokwa brand: a known subject matter expert and personality in the space, a unique name, and a colorful logo with an origin to Paul's Swahili roots. Now they just needed to apply these assets, in one way or another, to every type of channel and communication with their audience. From a branded website to branded merchandise, Bokwa would be consistent in the presentation of its corporate image. From personal posts on Paul's Facebook page to videos on a YouTube channel, the energy and excitement Paul had in the classroom would be amplified on social media.

• Goal: Build the Bokwa™ brand and promote the Bokwa program.

In a YouTube video titled, "What Is Bokwa?" Paul, his family, and instructors introduce the program to the world with the story of how they started in "trend-setting" Los Angeles,

California, and how they're advancing around the globe. The video leverages the brand origin (Los Angeles) and the countries (not cities) where they have already begun teaching with the instructors they certified based in the United Kingdom, Australia, New Zealand, and Taiwan.

     • Goal: Identify and certify instructors that could build a following for Bokwa.

Other target markets were identified in the video that mapped out the growth for the company based on relationships with current instructors (South Africa, Malaysia, Poland, Slovenia, Spain, Brazil, Germany, and Norway), and it also gave notice to instructors outside the community that Bokwa was coming and there was an opportunity to join.

What the video started, the website would complete. The site included information about the program and what made it unique, information about Paul, testimonials from the instructors, and a link to enroll in certification programs to become a Certified Instructor. The Bokwa community would share the video, share the website, and share stories of success implementing Bokwa in their classroom. Students who enjoyed the program would tell their friends and the numbers would grow, class by class, to build the number of paying participants for each of the Certified Instructors.

     • Goal: Attract students to the Bokwa program and help them find an instructor.

All of the foundational components were in place, tested, and verified. Now it needed to scale. As the organization grew, so did the number of people who needed to communicate. Paul needed to communicate with more instructors, and the instructors needed to communicate with more students.

When we looked to other businesses that had similar communications requirements, we saw corporate websites with logins for instructors to access an Intranet: a web-based communications platform that provides secure access to business information. For students, we found public pages with links to events and search functionality for instructor classes and online registration. All of which was helpful, but all that took time and money to develop. Once it was created, there was training for the users, and support for the instructors as new classes and students joined a program.

We knew that we needed a communications platform that would enable Bokwa to share content with the instructors, and that would enable instructors to share content with their students. We also needed to expose the public to the program and provide a way for them to learn more.

4. Selecting Social Media

In selecting social media, we started where Paul had already built an audience of instructors and students: Facebook and YouTube. He was comfortable on the platform, it worked for the type of content he had to share, and the personal relationships he had developed provided a referral network that was working.

The instructors were also on Facebook, using their profiles to demonstrate their focus on fitness and to communicate with students. They shared Paul, they shared Bokwa, and they shared pictures, video, and insights from every class.

Students who were already on Facebook were connected to instructors, and as the content trickled down, they shared with their friends along with comments and endorsements, which expanded the reach of the message: Bokwa was here, and everybody was having a great time.

5. Building Engagement

When we started working on a strategy for engagement, we couldn't help but notice two things: everyone in the audience was already on Facebook, and they were already using it, one way or another, to communicate. The communications platform we had been looking for was already in place, and it didn't cost a dime to develop. What it would take was structure, and what it would provide is engagement.

A Facebook fan page was created for Bokwa; a corporate brand page to be the focal point for information about the business, the leader (Paul), the program and the achievements of the company.

A fan page was created for each country as the focal point for the activity within each of the geographical locations. Denoted by its international country code (US, UK, AU, NZ,

TW, etc.), the pages were easily identified in Facebook search by the people looking for their country page and labeled in the profile picture for reassurance they had landed on the right page.

Facebook groups were created for each of the countries, as well, for the internal communications required between instructors. Using the closed group privacy settings allowed leaders to manage who has access to the group, and who does not. Updates, events, certifications, promotions, and best practices: everything necessary to build the brand in the country, and everything an instructor needed to build their business.

Instructors supported the corporate page by sharing the corporate content, and they supported their country page by engaging with the audience (students and prospects) who were looking to learn more, join the events, and share their experiences. Instructors engaged with one another at the local level to create excitement around the new programs, new students, and new opportunities to join the instructors respective programs (generating revenue for the instructors while attracting new people to the certification programs).

The company supported the engaged instructors reinforcing their commitment to support their people in the field, offering words of encouragement, acknowledging success in building class size, and publicly recognizing the best of the best.

6. Communications Planning

As lessons were learned and models of best practices were identified, we developed a communications plan to specifically support the goals of the program. Each post, every status update, and any of the content that was shared:

- Build the Bokwa™ brand and promote the Bokwa program.

Each page was branded according to the corporate guidelines we established allowing us to easily add new pages as they were needed. As one cover photo was updated, all were updated to maintain a visual interest in the pages upon arrival. When corporate added a new certification, the link was shared globally, across all pages, creating a channel of communication unmatched by any other media. When the media provided a story of success in one country, the link was shared with every other country demonstrating the global reach of the Bokwa program and providing an opportunity for every instructor to start another conversation with students and prospects.

- Identify and certify instructors that could build a following for Bokwa.

During those conversations, students who demonstrated an interest to learn how they could become instructors were identified and assigned to current instructors in the region providing a "next step" (literally) for prospects.

• Attract students to the Bokwa program and help them find an instructor.

Students joined the conversation, which exposed Bokwa to their friends, who saw their recent activity. When they were tagged in a picture or a post, this increased the inquiries leading to more business for the instructor and the company.

7. Measuring Performance

The measurement tools within Facebook provided more than enough data to measure the performance of this program. As Facebook Insights expanded, so did the data available for making decisions.

The company page provided quantitative data, like the number of fans, their location (by country), gender, age, and the types of content the audience engaged most. Every comment, like, or share could be traced back to the individual—we could get as much data as we needed to determine the success of this page.

The country pages provided the same, on a more localized level (if you consider a country to be local). The audience engagement on these pages provided a link to the leads instructors need to grow their class sizes, and the leads the company needed to increase the number of instructor certifications.

The Instructor pages provided a marketing and sales tool for the instructors to put their mark on their classes while supporting the company goals. The trickle down made it to the instructors as the interest grew, both from the interest from their colleagues in instructor opportunities and their class sizes grew impacting revenue where it mattered most: in their pocket.

Side Note: The innovation in this story is in the use of Facebook as the infrastructure for corporate communications. The vulnerability in the strategy was the lack of control with the channel. When Facebook made changes to its system, privacy, or functionality we had no control. - kp

Reference

Photo courtesy of Bokwa Fitness as retrieved 10-7-2015: http://pers.publicrelations.nl/2014/06/bokwa-the-latest-dance-fitness-craze-is-experiencing-explosive-growth-in-the-uk/

"What Is Bokwa" video as retrieved from https://www.youtube.com/watch?v=xK-odm1yyys

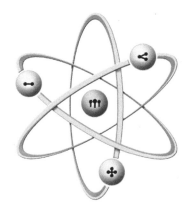

CHAPTER EIGHT

Non-Profit Organization Case Story:
Alliance Healthcare Foundation

Non-Profit Organization Case Story: Alliance Healthcare Foundation

Alliance Healthcare Foundation (AHF) advances health and welfare for those in need in San Diego and Imperial County, California. Through several types of grants, the foundation awards more than $2 million dollars each year to organizations impacting the health and wellness for the uninsured and underinsured.

We had recently rebranded the foundation to better represent the grantees funded through its grants: from organizations impacting homelessness to those in the education field, from food banks to non-profits in the technology space. The Executive Director and Program Director of AHF were active in the community, and their posts, pictures, and videos from meetings, on-site visits, and cause conferences were well received when featured on social networking, content sharing, and collaboration sites.

We had a strong foundation to build upon.

History: We had been working with Alliance for about six months when Executive Director Nancy Sasaki added an initiative to announce the 2012 Mission Support Grant (one of their flagship grants) awardees to our communications plan. After reviewing 80 applicant videos, the Board and Blue Ribbon Panel had selected 16 projects for funding. In total, more than $1,000,000 would be invested in advancing health and wellness within San Diego and Imperial Counties in Southern California.

In the past, the foundation had sent letters to awardees congratulating them on their selection. Foundation leaders met recipient leadership during a private luncheon, and thus concluded the interaction. Nancy had been adding up the budgets for this process and was surprised how much had been spent on letters and a lunch. The investment far exceeded her impression of the traditional event and its effectiveness in generating any interest outside of the attendees.

Today: Nancy had been very active in the community since her appointment and had been very open to re-addressing everything we worked with her on at Alliance. We'd had "fun" with other projects like the re-branding, the stationery system—even live-streaming the Funding Forum event.

Nancy asked, "What if we did something fun this year to announce the grantees?"

Vision: In thinking about the communication—announcing the awards to the grantees— we thought about the other ways people are notified they have been awarded. "What if we gave them giant checks, like Publisher's Clearinghouse?" I always loved the reaction people had to receiving a giant check and thought it could be a step up from just the letter. Nancy laughed along with us, and in a moment of creativity exceeding reality, she quickly added, "And what if we showed up with cameras just like the Prize Patrol?"

We stopped laughing—we were thinking. What If we did?

We continued with "what-ifs" as we drafted what each video would include. Like the Prize Patrol, a camera crew, a giant check, and an official representative announcing, "Congratulations, you've just won" would surprise recipients! Since the signature on the check came from the Executive Director, we reasoned she should also present the check.

As the presentation unfolds, viewers would expect to see the reaction of the awardees and to hear a few words on what they're going to do with their grant. Locations for each presentation would likely be their place of operations, providing an opportunity to share a glimpse into the programs themselves, and maybe even the people they serve.

Nancy accepted the challenge and suggested we include Alliance's newly appointed Program Officer, Sylvia Barron, since each project would be working with her directly. Comparisons to "Kathie Lee and Hoda" continued the laughs but also facilitated discussions on direction and mood of the presentation. We agreed we wanted to have fun with the approach, but we also wanted to be perceived as respectful and professional. We all, of course, would be representing Alliance Healthcare Foundation.

Issues: Nancy was getting excited about the idea, but the investment was adding up to be more than a luncheon—how could this investment make sense? How could we create enough ROI to proceed?

Production would require a 16-location shoot. Sixteen "meetings" would have to be scheduled with project leaders to get the right people on camera, and coordinating multiple executives from each organization would be critical. If we could consolidate the 16 shoots into a couple days, maybe we could do it—but what about editing 16 videos?

1. Identifying the Goals

For the time and dollars, the goal of the video series would have to provide more than just replacing the letter.

- Announce the award to grantees.
- Capture the award presentations to share with the public.
- Represent the Board and Foundation while demonstrating Alliance "in the community."
- Educate the public about the issues in the community and how each grantee would. be using foundation dollars to make an impact on the people they serve.

Once the primary goals of the video series were considered, we looked at secondary goals and identified an even greater return:

- Attract more qualified applicants for the next year of grant applications.

These videos would demonstrate Alliance in the community long after the announcement period ended. Viewers from the grantee organization, their colleagues, and the people they serve would be introduced on-screen to two key people from the foundation in a positive environment. This would make them more accessible, provide a face and a name to contact, and plant a seed of thought about applying for a grant.

2. Understanding the Audience

With the active AHF social media platform we had developed, we discussed the audiences who would view, and hopefully share, our content: grantees, applicants, project managers, grant writers, service coordinators, government, media, and people in the community.

Each audience was represented in the fans, followers, and subscribers to one or more of Alliance social media profiles.

We were very familiar with the demographics of the organizations in San Diego working in health and wellness. The foundation had been funding for several years, and the new leadership had been very active at earlier positions at related organizations.

There was a need for a greater understanding of Imperial County since Alliance had not funded as many organizations based there in the past. The two-hour drive through the mountains did very much to divide the region and to limit the information and relationships that had been more easily created in San Diego.

Understanding the psychographics of both audiences seemed to reveal one thing they did have in common: understanding the foundation behind the grant and identifying the right type of funding. In survey results, respondents had identified concerns about not knowing enough about the people behind the foundation*. They were often concerned about the conditions of the grant: What could they do with the money, and what couldn't they do with the money?

3. Creating the Strategy

We designed a model in pre-production to minimize how much time we'd need on-site for each award—at least an hour. A cameraman, director, and a soundman would provide a professional level of production and support for our inexperienced on-camera talent. A checklist of shots necessary to produce the video would keep things moving quickly and would help our crew stay on schedule.

A simple graphics package would brand the video, help the presentation of on-the-run video, and the lower-thirds could share additional information while adding a sense of production to each video. Underneath it all, an upbeat music bed could add an audio signature to keep it all moving along for the viewer, increasing the length of time they would watch. At the end of each video would be our call to action, "To learn more about our grant applications, visit our website."

Side Note: Although this strategy had professional resources for content development, none of this success would have been possible without the personal contribution from Nancy Sasaki and Sylvia Baron, and the committment from the AHF staff in supporting the program. - kp

The shot opens with the camera wide, showing the organization receiving the grant. On-screen are our hosts, giant check in hand, delivering a lively and likeable, "Hi, I'm Nancy Sasaki, Executive Director of Alliance Healthcare Foundation," as she and Sylvia announce where they are located, why they are there, and how much they are awarding the organization.

   • Goal: Capture the award presentations to share with the public.

"Let's go inside," initiated the move into the building as we asked to locate the leadership of the new grantee. As the camera made its way down the hall, up the stairs, and into the offices and conference rooms where their leaders would be found, we would build a sense of excitement leading up to the moment where we would announce, "Congratulations, you've been awarded a grant from Alliance Healthcare Foundation!"

   • Goal: Represent the Board and Foundation while demonstrating Alliance
     "in the community."

Varying collections of Executive Directors, Program Directors, Board members, and volunteers would gather to receive the giant check. With some well-prepared questions, Nancy would facilitate an interview with representatives who could speak to what they do and to how the grant would benefit those they served.

• Goal: Educate the public about the issues in the community and how each grantee would be using foundation dollars to make an impact on the people they serve.

The call to action would be: "To learn more about this organization, visit their grantee profile on our website." Many of the grantees did not have websites or the ability to present themselves to the public. By developing a consistent grantee profile page on the site, Alliance could present the grantees equally, showcasing the award video and its application video (a requirement of the application) while repurposing information from their application form, like their mission statement, pictures of their facility, or programs and contact information (which was often difficult for the public to find).

4. Selecting Social Media

We had developed a social media platform for Alliance as part of the rebranding, including a YouTube channel, a Google+ page, a Twitter profile, a LinkedIn company page, a Pinterest profile, and a Facebook fan page.

5. Building Engagement

Each of the social media sites provided different types of engagement opportunities. Each video was uploaded to a playlist on the Alliance YouTube channel. Each used a common structure in the title which featured the organization's name and included a description, links, and keywords. All subscribers to the channel would be notified of the upload, and visitors would see the new addition upon their review of recent uploads. Each visitor would see a new video featured on the channel.

Links to the YouTube videos were shared with its circles and publicly on Google+, including posts with hyperlinks to the organizations that had pages on Google+. We included hashtags (#health, #wellness, #grants) as applicable to interject our content into larger conversations within existing content streams.

Google+ did not attract a big audience or receive as much engagement as others, but the SEO benefit has always been thought worthwhile in return for repurposing messages, links, hashtags, and content.

Twitter also used links, hashtags, and a shorter version of the post to manage the 140 characters available. Once the grantee was followed, their handle (@username) created a hyperlink to their account, leading our audience to the grantees in the hopes of building their following. This tactic also notified the grantee that our message had been posted on their behalf for the purpose of initiating a response: those that were actively managing their communications did.

The LinkedIn Company Page was gaining followers, and it represented the foundation in a more traditional business manner. The leaders of the larger health and wellness organizations would see the posts as well.

Pinterest repurposed the still images from the albums with description copy and links to the videos. The demographics of Pinterest (mostly women) made it of particular interest, since a majority of professionals in health and wellness are women.

Our most active audience had been on Facebook, and this trend continued as we uploaded each video directly to the Facebook fan page. Historically, we have seen (and read reports) of greater engagement with videos uploaded directly compared to links to YouTube. According-ing to a report from Social Bakers (O'Reilly, 2014), "Facebook videos were simply 'more nat-ural' to share and interact with than YouTube videos. They appear in the news feed, which is a key discovery platform. Discussions in the comments are (for the most part) with your friends rather than strangers. And Facebook also provides a bigger video preview image through the news feed than the small preview boxes you get on YouTube."

The same post content was repurposed for the other audiences; hashtags and hyperlinks were included as well. Again, the purpose was to message our audience, to engage the grantee, and to get in front of their audiences (where posted messages were displayed to the recipient's audience automatically).

The embedded code provided from YouTube for each video would be used to include the video in the grantee profile page on the Alliance web site (http://AllianceHF.org). We also included the YouTube video each grantee submitted with their online application. Information from the application, like the mission statement, contact, and overview provided a body of text that presented them quite nicely. A picture gallery across the bottom provided still images that continued to tell their story.

Each grant initiated engagement with an organization—a reason for the people from each business to collaborate. The video fueled the engagement by funding the organization, introducing its key leaders to our community, and providing our content to them as marketing content (many of whom never had such resources).

Leading by example, Alliance would share the content with each organization, providing new content for their growing social media efforts and showcasing examples of how to best present it to their audiences. The on-boarding process would also include "liking," "following," and "subscribing" to AHF's social properties to provide ongoing examples of how to use social media.

6. Communications Planning

The COMM Plan™ started by looking at the assets from the investment: 16 three-minute videos demonstrating Alliance's Executive and Program Directors interacting with our grantees in the community.

One video would be posted each business day, providing 16 days of unique content on the AHF editorial calendar. Shooting in HD, each three-minute video provided high-resolution digital still frames to create grantee-named photo albums for each awarded organization. Behind–the-scenes photos would provide additional insights into the hard work and commitment from Alliance to be in the community.

With each video, the Alliance social media platform was leveraged to share its photos and links to the organization's social media. Additional posts included links to their websites and their grantee profiles on the AHF site, cumulatively providing thousands of impressions to the local community.

A distributed press release would be the final step in announcing the grantees. With so much traffic on the Alliance website/social media and the scheduled engagement from our 16 new grantees, the media would arrive in the midst of it all.

7. Measuring Performance

Using PRWeb, the press release titled, "Alliance Healthcare Foundation Uses Social Media to Announce 2012 Mission Support Grant Awards" targeted San Diego media. The release received 31,632 impressions over 26 days, resulting in 683 total reads.

- Goal: Announce the award to grantees.

The Facebook fans were up 200 percent, and its social media reach grew each day, nearing 100,000 Facebook impressions in just one week! The YouTube videos have received hundreds of views and were being viewed on smartphones and tablets as much as they were being seen on the website. The LinkedIn company page has received 13 recommendations for its Mission Support Grants, messaging that will be important in encouraging applicants for next year's process. The following year, an additional 20 grantees provided recommendations for the Mission Support Grants, totaling 33 grantee recommendations.

- Goal: Attract more qualified applicants for the next year of grant applications.

In testing the process models each year and comparing the performance of each, we have continued to improve the number of applicants for grants year by year:

- Total applicants in 2012: 80
- Total applicants in 2013: 102
- Total applicants in 2014: 106
- Total Applicants in 2015: 114

From the qualitative, we could review any of the 33 recomendations recieved from grantees. We also look to the recommendation from the Executive Director in reviewing the completed program:

"All I had was an idea of what I wanted to create and [the team] was able to take those thoughts and make it all a reality. Not only that but [the process] brought new ideas and creativity to expand and built my confidence so I didn't have to worry along the way. The end result was above and beyond my original idea and expectations. 150% satisfied with the results!"
 – Nancy Sasaki, Executive Director, Alliance Healthcare Foundation

References

* AHF External Survey Results (2011, March). Alliance Healthcare Foundation.
* O'Reilly, L. (2014, December 9). Facebook Video Is Driving YouTube Off Facebook. Retrieved December 1, 2014, from: http://www.businessinsider.com/facebook-video-v-youtube-market-share-data-2014-12

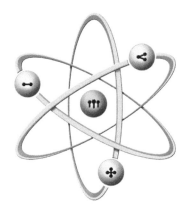

EPILOGUE

A Call to Action

In the end, Satellite Marketing is a metaphor to understand how social media works and where the opportunities are for a business to create engagement.

As history shows, Marketing has changed because people change. Business will continue to learn more about the people who buy their products and services and they will change. People will continue to buy from companies who meet their needs as they change. Both will continue to want to communicate with one another and social media provides common ground.

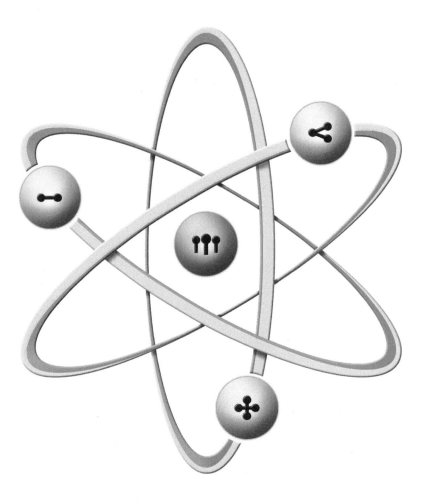

Like other communications before, social media has gained enough mass and adoption and will remain a channel. With the technological integration of our rapidly evolving digital lives, social media is part of how people communicate. No media in history has yet to regress (Print never died) and we should not expect that social media would either. As long as people and business use social media, it will remain part of the integrated communications plan.

At the micro level, the popularity of social media will continue to change. The Facebook and LinkedIn and Twitter of today were the MySpace, Plaxo, and AOL of yesteryear. Look for continuous variations on these themes, but at the macro level, keep it simple: social networking, content sharing, and collaboration. When something comes along that doesn't fit in one of these buckets, look for an update to this book.

The reasons to use social media, to me, seem to greatly out-weigh the reasons not to use social media for my business. You will have to determine if this is the case for your business, just like if you were deciding to give a speech, send an email or have salesperson call a list of prospects from a call center. There is an inherent risk in business communications, especially in regulated industries, and in using regulated methods of communications. As professionals have learned in all types of media in all types of industries, manage the communications and you can mitigate the risk.

Using a proven process helps to mitigate the risk in using social media.

Satellite Marketing always starts with identifying the goals. Whether they're SMART or the result of team collaboration, or any other process you find for goal planning, following the process and complete the exercise. When you do, you'll know you have thought of enough different things in enough different ways that you were able to make an informed decision. That's all you need to believe to move forward.

Understanding your audience will help you decide how your goals could include them, and how social media could help in creating engagement to reach those goals. The more you know about the people in your audience, the more you will know what to say and how to say it to these people to help you reach your goals.

Creating a strategy that gets an audience to purposefully engage comes from knowing your business—your real business—and the others with which you compete for time, mindshare, or money. From SWOT to Blue Ocean, or any of the other ideation processes, move through a process and complete the exercise to believe that you have thought of enough different things in enough different ways to make an informed decision about your strategy. Remember, a plan is not a purchase agreement for results. The formulation of strategy will be best evaluated by measuring its success over time.

Selecting which social media to implement is important, and starting with what your audience already uses is the easiest course of action; they're already there. Getting people to use another platform has to address the "what's in it for me" enough to motivate. Creating the perception starts with the selection of media. Marshall McLuhan famously said, "The medium is the message," meaning "the form of a medium embeds itself in the message, creating a symbiotic relationship by which the medium influences how the message is perceived." Secondly, the profiles presented extend the perception ultimately shaping who you are in the eyes of your audience. Remember, there's a lot of different people in the audience: Make sure everybody gets what they're coming for.

Building engagement will take time, or money, or both. Attracting an audience that helps you meet your goals (usually) doesn't just happen, and knowing your audience will help you start a conversation. Your strategy will need to demonstrate how you will hold their attention, over time, to reach your goals. Understanding this process and measuring engagement will help you improve this process. Managed correctly, the result will be relationships with people that generate social capital, and equity to be accessed as needed.

Communications planning will provide the roadmap of what to do and when to do it. Building models—a week, a month, and a year—will map actions to goals and insures your activity on social media is purposeful (and not a time sink). Develop different models, test against another, and find out what works—and why. Follow the COMM Planning process and complete the exercise to know that you have thought of enough different things in enough different ways to make an informed decision about your communications.

Measuring performance is mission critical. It provides the answer to the question, "How are we doing?" and direction on where to go in the future. Although the "what" you measure may be unique, the "why" is all the same: To answer, "Is what we're doing bringing us closer to or farther away to our goal?"

From the first time I drew concentric circles on a whiteboard (2007) to the debut of this book in my classroom at San Diego State University (2015), and through the countless workshops, presentations, and clients in between, people of all backgrounds and disciplines have told me the concept of satellites moving constantly around an audience helped them "get it," and I hope you now do too.

A Call to Action

During my doctoral studies in Duquesne University's School of Education, then Program Director Dr. Larry Tomei taught us that a teacher's job is to set up their students for success. He taught us to provide the knowledge, resources, and experiences necessary for each of our students to prosper in the programs of our design. It has been my intent to set you up for success by taking you through everything I think you should know to develop a social media platform for your business and to create engagement with your audience.

You have new knowledge, wisdom, and process. All of the resources referenced in the book are online at SatelliteMarketing.com.

The case studies provided herein are stories of how different types of businesses have successfully used social media to create engagement, and I have hundreds more. If you're interested in learning more, follow @SatelliteMktg on Twitter.

If you have questions about the material, just ask. As an educator, I am committed to my students. Consider yourself one of my many, and let me know what you need to succeed. Connect with me on LinkedIn and introduce yourself and let me know how I can help.

Now, let's get started.- kp

References

Marshall McLuhan, *The Medium Is the Message*: As retrieved: http://en.wikipedia.org/wiki/ The_medium_is_the_message

Kevin Popović | Founder, Author, Speaker, Teacher

@KEVINPOPOVIC

"If you have questions about the material, just ask. As an educator, I am committed to my students. As a colleague, I'm here to help."

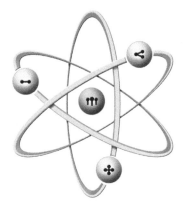

GLOSSARY

Terms and Definitions

Account Management – A service provided by agencies to clients that includes the management of the business between the two companies as well as the communications planning and creative development requirements of the client.

Account Planning – A process that considers the quantitative and qualitative information of target audiences during the development of a communications plan for a business. Also referred to as brand planning or strategic planning.

Account Service – The department within an agency that is responsible for the day-to-day management of client interests and resources. Roles include Account Executives and Project Managers.

Advertising – A form of communication used to educate, inform, or persuade an audience to respond to a call to action. Advertising channels include television, radio, outdoor, print, and online. Most frequently, advertising is used to move consumers to purchase a product or service or to respond to a call to action.

Advocates – Consumers whose brand loyalty moves them to suggest a product or service to others.

Apps – An abbreviation for a specific application that provides a useful task to the user. Apps are commonly found on smartphones and tablet computers and other mobile devices. Available through distribution platforms, apps are downloaded to the target device.

Audience – A specific group of people within a target market identified to sell a product or service. An audience is described by combining age, gender, marital status, education, geographic location, etc. Identifying an appropriate target audience is considered the most critical activity in communications.

B2B – An acronym for "business to business," B2B describes the business transactions between businesses, like a wholesaler and a retailer.

B2C – An acronym for "business to consumers," B2C describes the common retail business transaction between a business and the end user.

Bandwidth – The rate of data transmitted over a network measured in bits per second (bps), sometimes used to refer to a team or individual's available capacity to complete a task or project.

Branding - A marketing practice that involves the creation of a name, term, symbol, or design that identifies a product or service and separates it from similar products or services. Often considered the most valuable asset of an organization, companies manage their brands to maximize their value in the marketplace.

Clients – Individuals or organizations that contract an agency or expert for communications services.

Collaboration – A type of social media that enables people to create a social network and to share content for a purpose—a small project, particular interests, or on a larger scale to create social capital or for capital gain.

COMM Plan™ – A process modeling methodology, based on best practices, to facilitate the development of an integrated marketing communications plan.

Communications – The meaningful transmission of messages using speech, visuals, signals, writing, or behavior between two or more people. Communication requires a sender, message and a receiver and may be synchronous (like a conversation) or asynchronous (like an advertisement).

Communitivity – The use of interpersonal skills, technology, and connectivity to facilitate the development of a personal community. Defined by Kevin Popović, personal communitivity can be thought of as the measure of the concurrent and overlapping circles of activity, both online and on-site, to create a presence.

Consumer – An individual or group that purchases a product or service produced or provided by a company for personal use.

Content Sharing - A type of social media that enables people to share information and electronic media including text, documents, pictures, video, music, multimedia, etc. Content sharing sites also provide the ability to construct content, to create an archive of content, and to monitor its ongoing development.

Conversation Prism – Developed by Brian Solis, the Conversation Prism is a visual map of the social media landscape. It's an ongoing study in digital ethnography that tracks dominant and promising social networks and organizes them by how they're used in everyday life.

Originally developed in 2008, the work has been updated as social media has evolved.

Corporate Identity – The overall image of a business, product, or service in the minds of its audiences, including customers, clients, investors, or employees. Commonly, a corporate identity is recognized to include the name and logo, as well as an emotional connection, i.e., a consumer "likes" a product.

Corporate Propaganda – Intentionally manipulative communications spread by businesses. Often used to manipulate the stock market or in political advocacy. Media manipulation is the most common form of corporate propaganda.

Cost per thousand impression (CPM) – A simple and widely used method of comparing the cost effectiveness of two or more alternative media vehicles. It is the cost of using the media vehicle to reach 1,000 people or households. The CPM of any vehicle is computed by dividing the cost of placing a specific ad or commercial in the media vehicle by the vehicle's audience size and multiplying the result by 1,000.

Creative Director – A leadership role in graphic design and advertising agencies, the creative director works with copywriters, art directors, graphic designers, photographers, programmers, etc., to develop client communications.

Crowdsourcing – The practice of obtaining services, generating ideas, or developing content by soliciting participation from a group of people, usually from an online community.

Demographics – The study of total size, sex, territorial distribution, age, composition, and other characteristics of human populations; the analysis of changes in the make up of a population.

Design - The conception of a plan or convention that influences and guides the construction of an object or a system, sometimes used as a synonym for graphic design.

Digital Strategist – A person within the marketing department who leads the development of digital initiatives for an organization. Their focus includes customer intelligence, website development, social media, mobile, e-commerce, search engine optimization, and advertising.

E-Commerce – Also known as electronic commerce, e-commerce is an industry that facilitates the buying and selling of products and services using electronic systems, like the Internet. E-commerce includes the use of mobile commerce, electronic funds transfer, online transaction processing, inventory management, and customer management.

Facebook – An online social media networking service founded by Mark Zuckerberg in 2004. With more than 1 billion users (March 2013), Facebook is the largest social media network.

Flickr – An image and video hosting website and community acquired by Yahoo! in 2005. The service is most commonly used by bloggers to embed photographs and share them across social media.

Fortune 500 Company – A list compiled by *Fortune* magazine ranking the top 500 public corporations by gross revenue.

Foursquare – A local search and discovery service mobile app that provides a personalized local search experience for its users.

Frequency- The number of times a person, household, or member of a target market is exposed to a media vehicle or an advertiser's media schedule within a given period of time. This number is usually expressed as an average frequency (the average number of exposures during the time period) or as a frequency distribution (the number of people exposed once, twice, three times, etc.).

Google+ – A social networking and identity service that is owned and operated by Google Inc.

Impression – One view or display of an ad. Ad reports list total impressions per ad, which tells you the number of times your ad was served by the search engine when searchers entered your keywords (or viewed a content page containing your keywords).

Integrated Marketing Communications – A planning process designed to assure that all brand contacts received by a customer or prospect for a product, service, or organization are relevant to that person and consistent over time.

Internet - A general term used to describe a global network of computers used to transmit information. The most familiar aspect of the Internet is the World Wide Web, which consists of various interlinked Web sites.

LinkedIn - A social networking service centered on business professionals. LinkedIn allows professionals to connect to other professionals, and view their credentials, work experience, skills, and network of peers.

Marketing - The process of communicating the value of a product or service to customers within a marketplace for the purpose of creating a sale. This includes the use of science to select target markets by using market analysis and segmentation as well as understanding consumer behavior.

Marketing Director – The corporate executive that leads and coordinates marketing efforts for a company or organization. This role is often seen as of prime importance within the organization, providing information that helps guide other departments toward a common goal.

Marketing Mix – The mix of controllable marketing variables that the firm uses to pursue the desired level of sales in the target market. The most common classification of these factors is the four-factor classification called the "Four Ps"—price, product, promotion, and place (or distribution). Optimization of the marketing mix is achieved by assigning the amount of the marketing budget to be spent on each element of the marketing mix to maximize the total contribution to the firm. Contribution may be measured in terms of sales or profits or in terms of any other organizational goals.

Mass Media – The collective term for communication mediums designed to reach large audiences, including broadcast, film, video games, radio, Internet, print, and outdoor media.

Media – A generic term for communication medium, sometimes used synonymously with mass media. Also used to describe the storage and transmission of information or data.

Media Buying – A process in advertising whereby media real estate is obtained for both optimal placement and optimal price. The main responsibility of a media buyer is to identify the best price and placement to reach the target audience.

Media Convergence – The evolution of media and mediums to evolve toward a singular common platform.

Media Fragmentation – A trend toward an increasingly diverse number of channels and mediums for consuming media resulting in the decreasing number of people in each audience. For media buyers, this means they must purchase more advertising channels to reach the needed number of customers than before.

Media Planning – The process that an agency uses to determine the best combination of media to achieve a client's goals or objectives.

Metrics – The collection of data related to the reach and effectiveness of communications efforts for the purpose of measurement and analysis.

Mobile – A category characterized by portable, battery-powered products, including cell phones, smartphones, and tablets.

Multimedia – Media and content that uses a combination of different content forms, including a combination of text, audio, still images, animation, video, or interactivity content forms.

MySpace – A social networking service known for its emphasis on music. From 2005 to 2008, MySpace was the most visited social networking site in the world. It is credited with significantly influencing music, gaming, and the use of unique URLs for artists.

Networking – The process of developing a social network with others who share similar personal interests or business objectives using a profile, personal information, content, and online activity.

New Media – An abstract term that refers to digital media that rose to popularity after traditional media like television, radio, and print had been established.

Outsource – Contracting an internal business process outside of a company.

Permission Marketing – Refers to the process of getting a customer's permission to contact them with future marketing messages, usually via email; coined by Seth Godin.

Pinterest – A social photo-sharing website that allows users to create theme-based image collections. Users browse other boards for images and "re-pin" (share) images to create their own boards of interest.

Podcasting – A series of digital media episodes including audio and video. Users subscribe to content using web-syndication services and a computer or mobile device.

Post-production – The last stage of the production process for film, video, and photography during the production of motion pictures, films, television, radio, advertising commercials, audio recordings, photography, and other digital products.

Pre-production – The process of planning and preparing all of the elements used in the production of motion pictures, films, television, radio, advertising commercials, audio recordings, photography, and other digital products.

Process – A premeditated series of steps taken to achieve a result.

Production – The act of performing and recording motion pictures, films, television, radio, advertising commercials, audio recordings, photography, and other digital products.

Productivity – 1. (Economic definition) A measure of the economic output per unit of input of some resource, e.g., the economic output per hour of human labor. [Department of Labor Statistics] 2. (Environments definition) A ratio of output per unit of input employed. It is measured by the U.S. Bureau of Labor Statistics as output per hour and output per combined unit of labor and capital per hour (multifactor productivity) for the business sector as a whole and for its major subsectors.

Psychographics – Quantified psychological profiles of individuals, based on their attitudes and behavior, as defined by the Amsterdam-based European Society for Opinion Marketing and Research.

Public Relations - Also known as "PR," public relations is the development and management of information and opinion of an individual, business, or organization and the public via media and events.

Reach – The number of different persons or households exposed to a particular advertising media vehicle or a media schedule during a specified period of time. It is also called cumulative audience, cumulative reach, net audience, net reach, net unduplicated audience, or unduplicated audience. Reach is often presented as a percentage of the total number of persons in a specified audience or target market.

Research – The methodical search for insight into a topic or issue for the purpose of obtaining new information and making informed decisions.

Return on Investment – The perceived gain for the resources spent on an effort, return on investment typically refers to financial capital but can also refer to more abstract rewards like increased awareness and loyalty or the growth of a social good; also called ROI.

Rhetoric – The art of persuasion through speaking or writing.

Sales - The process of identifying a prospect, introducing a product or service, and creating an exchange for money.

Satellite Marketing – A process for developing an actionable social media strategy, based on goals. Social media sites and services can be developed to serve as marketing sub-stations, or "satellites" offering smaller, faster, more dynamic communications opportunities, engaging people where they are already engaged. Satellites are used in addition to, or in place of, traditional media as part of an integrated marketing communications plan.

Saturation – The diffusion of a product or service in the market, saturation is sometimes used to suggest over-saturation. The level of saturation can depend on variables like price, competition, and consumer purchasing power.

Search Engine Optimization (SEO) - The process of developing a marketing/technical plan to ensure effective use of search engines as a marketing tool. Typically consists of two elements. On a technical side, SEO refers to ensuring that a website can be indexed properly by the major search engines including keywords, content, and links. On the marketing side, SEO refers to the process of targeting specific keywords where the site should "win" in searches. This can be done by modifying a website to score well in the algorithms that search engines use to determine rank, or by purchasing placement with individual keywords. Often, SEO programs are a blend of several elements and strategies.

Slideshares - Slide-based presentations (such as a Microsoft PowerPoint presentation) formatted for online use and sharing.

Social Bookmarking - A centralized, online service enabling users to add, annotate, edit, and share bookmarks of web documents.

Social Capital – In social media, "social capital" refers to the total combined value of all social networks for a given person or business.

Social Media - People using content and technology to communicate within a social network.

Social Network – A collection of people using social media.

SWOT Analysis - A SWOT analysis is a structured planning method used to evaluate the strengths, weaknesses, opportunities, and threats involved in a project or in a business venture.

Target Audience – A specific group of people within a target market defined by demographics and psychographics.

Technological Convergence – The evolution of technological systems moving toward similar platforms and tasks.

Traditional Media – The collection of media that existed prior to the Internet, traditional media includes television, radio, film, music, newspapers, magazines, and books.

Tumblr – A short-form microblogging platform that allows users to post multimedia content. Purchased by Yahoo! in 2013 for $1.1 billion.

Twitter – A social networking site and microblogging service where users can send and receive posts, known as "tweets," which are limited to 140 characters.

Unique Selling Proposition – Also known as USP, unique selling proposition is a marketing concept developed by Rossar Reeves that proposed advertisers present unique propositions to the consumer to help convince them to convert brand choices.

Vendor – A person or company who offers a product or service to a company.

Veoh - An Internet TV company based in San Diego, California, which allows users to watch independent, user-created material as well as major studio productions.

Vimeo - A video-sharing site where users can upload, share, and watch videos.

WordPress – An open-source content management system (CMS) used for blogs and for websites, ranked as the most popular blogging system in the world (2013).

YouTube – A video-sharing website where users can upload, view, and share video using HTML5 technology to display user-generated movies, short films, educational programs, television shows, and music videos.

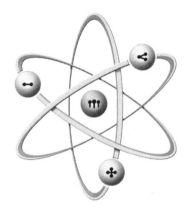

INDEX

Words and Phrases

Index

A